LIFE SKILLS
FOR
GUYS

"Tim Smith's love for families, his expertise and experience in working with youth, and his passion for ministry emerge on the pages of this book. It's a *must read* for parents with teens."

J. Otis Ledbetter
Chairman of board, Heritage Builders Association
Senior pastor, Chestnut Baptist Church

"This is life changing material! *Life Skills for Guys* is a very proactive and concrete way to mentor and be an influence to our kids. Our hearts and minds tell us we must proactively place spiritual deposit in our kids' lives. This book is a practical method of helping us do what our hearts want to do."

Jim Burns, Ph.D.
President, National Institute of Youth Ministry

LIFE SKILLS
FOR
GUYS

TIM SMITH

Cook Communications

Faith Parenting is an imprint of
Cook Communications Ministries, Colorado Springs, Colorado 80918
Cook Communications, Paris, Ontario
Kingsway Communications, Eastbourne, England

LIFE SKILLS FOR GUYS

Printed in the United States of America.

1 2 3 4 5 6 7 8 9 10 Printing/Year 04 03 02 01 00

Editor: Liz Duckworth
Cover Design: Dave Thomasin
Interior Design: Pat Miller

Library of Congress Cataloging-in-Publication Data
Smith, Tim.
    Life skills for guys / by Tim Smith
        p.cm.
    ISBN 0-7814-3406-8
        1. Teenage boys—Life skills guides. I. Title.

HQ797.S55 2000
305.235—dc21   00-027266

To my nephews—
Kevyn and Goeffrey

Check out more *Life Skills* at Tim Smith's website: Lifeskills.org

CONTENTS

HOW TO USE THIS BOOK

INSTRUCTIONS FOR TEENS AND PARENTS

Don't worry! This book isn't as scary as learning to drive. It's about learning to drive your life. And you don't even need a car!

Can you imagine trying to learn how to drive without ever being inside a car? Let's say you were raised by wolves on a desert island (just pretend, okay?), and you are rescued by the same Coast Guard Cutter that rescued Gilligan. *Finally!*

You are in the good old United States of America and you become the hit celebrity for all the daytime talk shows. "Wolf Boy Shares His Deep Tanning Secrets, tomorrow on 'This Day' show." You make all this money from your appearances. Wisely, you buy some clothes and lose the loincloth, but you still have thousands left over. *I will buy a car so I can drive to more TV studios,* you reason.

There is only one problem; you have only been in one car—the taxi that brought you from the dock. You have limited car experience. You don't know much about cars. *Do they all have a meter? Do they all smell? Do they all have photos of men with very long names on the visor?*

You would be foolish to try to gain car experience by yourself. You really would be a fool if you tried to buy a car with your limited car experience.

What should Wolf Boy do?

He should get a car mentor—someone to guide him around the potholes and cesspools of the automotive world. He should find someone who has actually driven and owned a car.

Being a teenager can be like learning to drive; it offers lots of new, exciting, and frightening experiences. Here's my advice:

Don't attempt being a teenager alone!

You wouldn't try driving without proper instruction (okay, well, you shouldn't!).

Life Skills is a book that will help you learn to drive through life, especially those next few years while you are on the teenage turnpike. The idea is to help you connect with your parent or another caring adult.

This is a book on *mentoring.* Mentoring is *connecting youth with adults from whom they can learn and receive coaching, encouragement, support, and guidance.*

You may be a parent of a teen, a youth worker, a concerned adult, or a curious teen. If you know anything about today's youth culture, I am sure you would agree: *Teens need mentors.* Teens are growing up in a culture that is increasingly dangerous for them.

Teens are hurried. Our culture is not comfortable with the teenage years, so we rush our children toward adulthood. Teens are copying the frantic pace of their parents. Today's teens are being robbed of their innocence, exposed to things that are intended only for adults. They are unprepared and overexposed to the harsh realities in life. They need the protection and guidance of a caring adult mentor, whether that is a parent or youth worker.

Teens are hassled. Teens are devalued in our society. Many feel they have no place and have been written off as *unnecessary* or *a nuisance.* They are too old to be considered "adorable," yet they are still dependent on adults. They are not ready to make positive contributions to society, but they want their independence. The confusion of being in this in-between place leaves them feeling hassled. They need clear steps toward adulthood and rites of passage that direct and celebrate their maturing.

Teens are hushed. They are lacking a voice. Their parents are busy with jobs, activities, commitments, mortgages, cell phones, and e-mails. They are drowning in information. With the flood of data, it is easy to silence or ignore our teenagers. We lack advocates for our youth. We need adults to speak up for and speak into the lives of our youth. A mentor is a caring adult who values kids enough to spend time with them and listen to them.

Teens are hostile. Across the country, we have seen evidence of hostile teens. The school and church shootings are the most dramatic examples.

Some may ask, "Why are these teens so hostile?"

It is because when they are *hurried, hassled,* and *hushed,* they become *hostile.*

We, who care about teens, can do something about this situation. We can choose to connect with our sons. We can protect them from being hurried. We can value them and show them they have a valid place. We can listen to them and be advocates for their concerns.

Or we can ignore them and deal with the hostility which results.

WHAT'S IN IT FOR ME?

If you are a guy between eleven and sixteen, you should be asking, *What's in it for me? Why do I need a mentor?*

Answer: to help you develop and make wise choices.

For some of you, your parent can also be your mentor. But some teens will need mentors who aren't their parents.

When you study successful people from all kinds of careers, you will discover that they had one thing in common: *someone to mentor them when they were young.* Bottom line? If you want to be successful, you will need a mentor.

Life is too risky to try to navigate without a mentor.

WHOSE JOB IS IT?

We are in a new millennium. *We need a new approach to developing our teens.* The old approach simply does not work. Many churches are still running their youth ministries on an approach shaped in the fifties. It was a program-centered model that separated adults from youth, keeping parents and their teens disconnected.

We need a new approach; one that encourages connecting the generations.

According to Scripture, the primary nurturers should be parents:

> Hear, O Israel! The LORD is our God, the LORD alone. And you must love the LORD your God with all your heart, all your soul, and all your strength. And you must commit yourselves wholeheartedly to these commands I am giving you today. Repeat them again and again to your children.

> Talk about them when you are at home and when you are away on a journey, when you are lying down and when you are getting up again. Tie them to your hands as a reminder, and wear them on your forehead. Write them on the doorposts of your house and on your gates (Deut. 6:4-9, NLT).

Our new approach is a people-centered, intergenerational model. It connects parents with teens and makes them their *primary spiritual nurturers.* The church will continue to support families in this role and be more active with teens whose parents can't mentor. Yet the church will remain in a supportive role. It is time for parents to be intentional about connecting with their teens. We can no longer drop them off at church youth group and think we have done our job.

SEVEN QUALITIES OF EFFECTIVE MENTORING

The purpose of *Life Skills* is to connect teens with parents (or other caring adults) in a mentoring relationship that prepares the teen to make wise choices. Our goal is to connect teens with parents. To help you get the most out of the mentoring relationship, remember the word *CONNECT.* The seven qualities spell it out:

▶ **C**onsistent. As a teen and as a mentor, you will need to be committed and dependable to meet together and work through *Life Skills.*

▶ **O**pen. Be authentic and honest about yourself and the issues dealt with in *Life Skills.* Be willing to take some risk as you dive in and discuss topics you have never discussed before.

▶ **N**urture. Be willing to provide an atmosphere of acceptance and willingness to grow. Both the mentor (parent) and the teen will be nurtured as they spend time in the process.

▶ **N**otice. Tune in to each other. Listen and observe nonverbal cues. Spend more time listening than talking, if you have a tendency to talk too much. Notice how the other person feels and displays his emotions.

▶ **E**ncourage. Pour courage into the other person by affirming him, believing in him, and supporting him. Create more encouragement by keeping certain discussions personal and confidential.

▶ **C**are. Demonstrate love by being patient, forgiving, understanding, and non-judgmental. Mentoring is more about care than it is about imparting information.

▶ **T**alk to God. Prayer is vital for effective mentoring. It keeps the focus right and helps us remember that we are not in this alone. Talking to God is a resource that gives us balance, perspective, and strength.

C.O.N.N.E.C.T. There you have it! Seven keys to making the most out of your mentoring relationship.

HOW DOES THIS WORK?

There are thirty-five chapters in *Life Skills*. The goal would be to get through all of them in one year. If you meet about once a week, you should be able to do this. *Both the mentor (parent) and the teen should have their own copies of Life Skills.* That way each can scribble in it, write in it, or decorate it the way he or she wants.

Each chapter has five parts:

▶ **Introduction**—sets up the topic, usually with true stories about teens.

▶ **Response**—five questions for the teen and parent to discuss based on the introduction.

▶ **A Letter To My Son**—letters to help launch discussions on the topic.

▶ **Journal Section**—a place for you to write your own letter. Parents may choose to use my letter as a model for their own. Teens may choose to respond to my letter or write one directed toward their parents.

▶ **Connection**—an activity that creatively strengthens the relationship between teen and parent. It usually involves making something or experiencing something together.

HOW DO I GET THE MOST OUT OF OUR MENTORING RELATIONSHIP?

1. Try to set up a regular time to get together; consider it an appointment, and try not to break it. Field testers suggest a standard time. For instance, many suggest Saturday breakfast before all of the day's activities begin. Others have found Sunday afternoon or evening works well.

2. Read the chapter before you get together. This is one more reason

why you need a copy for the parent *and* one for the teen. Sometimes it is just too difficult to share a book. Plus who wants to look for it in their messy room? (The parent's I mean!)

3. Don't expect it to always be serious. In fact, be flexible and ready to laugh.

4. Get together weekly and go through one chapter at a time. Start by catching up with what happened since the last time you met, then jump right into the questions from the Response section. If you want, you can make up additional questions on the material. You also may choose to read your letters to each other, but you don't have to. If you are in a place where you can pray, pray for each other, then go enjoy the Connection activity. You should be able to get through the discussion in about twenty to thirty minutes. The Connection time varies depending on the activity.

5. Make notes about your shared experiences in your book. It could become a real monument of treasured time together.

That's it! Everything you need to know to launch into a fun and rewarding experience. Thanks for picking up the book. It is my prayer that it will connect teens with parents and mentors in a unique way as they develop *Life Skills.*

Tim Smith
Thousand Oaks, CA

CHAPTER 1

NAVIGATING WITHOUT A COMPASS

H ey Tim, are you getting tired?"

"Yeah, getting stuck in the L.A. traffic took its toll on me."

"I'll drive for a while, if you want," Steve offered from the backseat.

I appreciated his offer. We had already been in the car for five hours, four high-school guys and myself. We were driving from San Diego to the High Sierras on a backpacking trip. It would be three fun-filled days in the beautiful back country, *if we ever got there!*

"Okay, I will pull over at the next spot and let you drive. I could use a nap."

I pulled off the freeway at the next off-ramp and climbed into the back.

"Where do I go?" asked Steve.

His question surprised me. *Didn't he automatically know where to go? After all, he is a guy!* "You don't know the way?"

"No. I've never been to the Sierras."

"All right. It's easy. Just follow this freeway until you get to highway 395 north."

"Then what?"

"Stay on that and that will take us right up to the mountains. Don't worry, I will wake up in a few hours before we get to the foothills."

"Don't worry about a thing. We will take care of it."

"Who are *we?*" I gestured to the other guys who were sacked out.

"I can handle it," Steve promised with confidence.

It had been a long day: gathering the supplies, packing the car, finishing all the details required before going out of town. I was exhausted, and

I had not even hiked yet! *A nap will feel great.* With Steve's, "I can handle it" on my mind, I dozed off to deep slumber. I dreamed of serene mountain streams.

The lights woke me up.

"Ah, Steve . . . hey, what, where?" I was trying to wake up. Ahead of us about ten miles was a giant halo of light. "What's that? Where are we?"

"Don't worry, Tim. Go back to sleep. Everything is okay."

I looked around the car; the other three guys were asleep. Steve was drumming on the dashboard with his right hand, steering with his left and humming along with the radio, "I Heard It Through the Grapevine" by Marvin Gaye.

"I hoyed it through the grapevine. Not much longer would you be mine. Oh, I hoyed it through—"

"STEVE! You missed the turnoff!"

"What do you mean, I followed your directions. I stayed on the freeway. You said you would wake up and you did."

My loud voice woke up the other guys. Who wiped their eyes and stared at the looming extravaganza of light ahead.

"You aren't taking us to the mountains. You missed the turnoff. You are taking us to VEGAS!"

"Las Vegas? Cool," offered Robert from shotgun.

"I can't believe you missed the turnoff. Remember *395 north*? It's going to take us forever to get there now."

A sheepish look washed over Steve's face, "Oh yeah, 395 north. Oops. Sorry." He glanced down at the speedometer.

It read ninety miles per hour.

Steve smiled, "At least we are making good time!"

"Yeah, we are making great time, but in the WRONG DIRECTION!"

I laugh now because it was just a backpack trip. But some people live their lives that way. They aren't sure where to go, so they pick up the pace. They get lost, but they don't ask for directions. They follow *The Guy Code*—which is a collection of unwritten, but understood rules of behavior for guys. One of those rules is: *Real men don't ask for directions.*

Steve, at eighteen years of age, had obviously mastered *The Guy Code.* He wouldn't dare wake us up or pull over to ask directions. *He was a guy* with a built-in Global Positioning Satellite chip embedded in his brain from birth!

When guys get lost, instead of pulling over and asking for directions (which is probably what most women would do and which is exactly why we don't), we speed up. We figure, *I will get un-lost faster if I speed up.*

Of course, all this does is guarantee a deeper level of lostness.

Some guys spend their whole lives running in circles, but trying to do it faster.

It's part of *The Guy Code.*

Some other highlights from the code include:

1. Never let them see you cry.
2. Never let them see you fail. *(Real men win.)*
3. Prove your worth with achievement and owning lots of cool stuff.
4. Don't depend on anyone but yourself.
5. Be aggressive. *(Real men make it happen. Wimps watch it happen.)*
6. Act like you know. NEVER read instructions, or *ask for directions.*

There have been times when I couldn't figure out how to assemble something. After a long time of struggling and yelling at it you would think: *Read the instructions, you idiot!*

That might be *you.*

But this is *me,* and I am a victim of the dreaded *Guy Code.*

When I can't assemble something, it is not simply an inconvenience; it is a challenge to my manhood! "I will make this fit. I am man—I will muscle it together!"

Guys, when your maleness is tested, it's usually wise to back off. I know that is difficult to do (it breaks *The Guy Code),* but when we try to prove our maleness, when we try to prove our strength and knowledge, it usually gets us into trouble. The "only-I-can-do-it" mentality generally backfires. When the focus is on ourselves, we are setting ourselves up. Pride comes before a fall.

As guys, we hate to admit our needs. Yet, that is whom God says we are—needy people, who sometimes get lost.

I know it is hard to swallow.

Real men don't ask for directions.

Real men are adventurers. We would rather stay on the expedition (stay lost) than stop and ask for directions. Stopping and asking for directions is admitting

we don't know everything. It reveals our vulnerability. It makes us look wimpy.
Needing to ask for directions is a brush with reality.

RESPONSE

1. Describe a time when you were lost
2. What are some of the feelings you have when you are lost?
3. What do you think about *The Guy Code?*
4. What are some ways we *act like we know?*
5. Can people be lost in life?

A LETTER TO MY SON

Dear Son,

I am looking forward to our talks on *Lifeskills.* I hope our time together will prepare you for life. I see so many young men navigating without a compass. They seem lost on the sea of life. They don't have a clue which way to sail or even which way is true north. We have many in a generation without a clear sense of direction. But I don't blame them; their parents haven't done much to point the way. Maybe *their* parents didn't, or else they didn't know how.

But we are going to be different. We are going to spend some time learning, laughing, and connecting.

I have to admit that I am nervous about your growing up. I don't want to lose you during your teenage years. That's why we have this book. I hope it provides us with a connection and builds some positive memories. I hope it helps you by providing guidance and reminding you that I love you. In my letters I want to give you a personal and warm view from where I sit in my recliner. You may not always agree with me, but that's okay; let's talk about it. I want to know your opinions and how you are feeling.

Today, I am thinking about being lost. It's easy to get lost. All you have to do is make a few wrong turns and you can forget where you are. But I am thinking about something more important than being lost on the road. I am thinking about walking through life lost. Living without purpose and direction. I hope this book and our conversations will be like helpful road signs that will guide you along the way. As you get older, I will tell you less and less what to do and where to go and how to do it. It's part of changing my parenting job from Director to Coach to Consultant.

A Scripture passage that has helped me when I was lost, or confused is Proverbs 3:5-7a: "Trust in the LORD with all your heart and lean not on your own understanding; in all your ways acknowledge him, and he will make your paths straight. Do not be wise in your own eyes."

If we rely only on our own understanding, knowledge, opinion, or experience, we can easily get sidetracked or lost. Sometimes we deceive ourselves thinking we know something, when we really don't. Instead of having 100 percent confidence in ourselves and our resources, we need to have 100 percent trust in God—with all of our heart. I have discovered that when I do this, when I let Him lead me, He does. "He makes my paths straight." That means even though it looks like a rough and curvy road ahead, God gets me through it.

But that last line is kind of a stinger: "Don't be wise in your own eyes." A fool is someone who thinks he knows it all. I don't want to be foolish. I want to keep learning. I want to ask for instruction.

I hope we can be open to learn from each other.

Love,
Dad

JOURNAL

Respond to the letter by writing your own thoughts here. Parents may want to use Tim's letter as a model for their own.

_____

_____

_____

_____

_____

_____

_____

_____

_____

⮞ CONNECTION ⮜

Asking for Directions

Blindfold your parent and have him or her ride in the backseat. Have someone drive you to a part of town that your parent won't recognize. In other words, see if you can get your parent lost. Remove the blindfold and see if your parent can find his or her way home. Just for fun, stop and ask for directions: first the teen and then, at another place, the parent. If you are still lost, have the driver show the way. Stop for a snack and discuss how it feels to be lost and what it was like for each person.

CHAPTER 2

BEING COACHABLE

He's talented, young, and rich. He made an early jump into the NBA and has marveled fans with his dazzling play. Kobe Bryant has added some sizzle to the Los Angeles Lakers. Coach Phil Jackson has said many favorable things about Kobe, but one sticks out in my mind: "He is *coachable*."

He could have said, "Excellent rebounder," "Playmaker," or "Has the ability to make the points and step up when we need it." But he didn't. He said, "Coachable."

Coachable. What does it mean?

One of the goals of *Life Skills* is to help teens become coachable. Being coachable means you can listen, observe, and learn. It doesn't mean you know nothing. It doesn't mean you can't do anything. Kobe Bryant can evade the double-team, spin, and do a reverse slam. I can't even comprehend how he makes his body move that way, let alone attempt any part of that move. He is an excellent player, but he is still *coachable*.

As long as you are coachable, you have the ability to improve.

That is what we want to do with *Life Skills*. We want to help improve your skills for life.

Even professional athletes, men and women who are at the top of their game and who get paid millions, have coaches.

You also need a coach and you need to be coachable.

Perhaps your coach is your parent, or a trusted adult friend. Maybe you call him your mentor. What you call him isn't as important as your relationship with him. There are two critical questions:

Can he coach?

Are you coachable?

Actually, the second question has more influence than the first. If you are coachable, it increases your coach's ability to help you.

THE JOB

A coach does more than teach. Can you imagine a basketball coach who lectured, showed highlights of NCAA basketball championships, and quoted John Wooden, but who never got out on the gym floor and practiced? Silly, isn't it?

A coach doesn't simply dump information on his players; he *shows* them how to play. He demonstrates with a real ball, with real players, in a real gym. A coach doesn't teach; he *trains.* Being a trainer involves physical connection and presence. It's hard to coach from a distance. Being a coach requires time and closeness.

As you get close to your coach he (or she) will train you in the fundamentals of life. Just as successful basketball has fundamentals like dribbling, passing, setting screens, shooting, and rebounding, so does life. To be good at life's fundamentals you will need a coach. You will also need to be *coachable.*

Being coachable means you are willing to be trained by your mentor or coach. We have defined mentoring as *connecting a young person with an adult from whom he can learn and receive coaching, encouragement, support, and guidance.*

For this to work connecting needs to occur. Connecting means having a commitment to a relationship. It's not simply a relationship for fun, but for learning. Connecting also means that it is mutual, that it goes both ways. In other words, both the teen and the mentor want the relationship and want to learn from each other.

Connecting means *that both mentor and teen have made a commitment to a learning relationship.* They have chosen to be together. The emphasis, of course, is that the teen will learn from the mentor, but most mentors do learn something from their protégés (or students).

The job of being a coach isn't the same as being a parent. A parent may choose to be a mentor, but not all mentors are parents. A parent does many of the same things that a coach or mentor does, but they aren't the same thing. In fact, a parent needs to change his or her style of parenting as children mature. When children are younger (up to age eleven or twelve), a parent may choose to be in the role of Director. In this role, he directs, disciplines, and *tells* his child what to do and when. This works when the child is little. It doesn't work so well when he turns twelve.

So what's a parent to do?

Become a *coach.*

Becoming a coach means showing not simply telling. It means debriefing and reviewing. Think of coaches reviewing videotape of last week's game. In the same way, we can learn by reviewing episodes in life. "What did you learn from that?" "What did you do well?" "What do you need to do differently?"

HUMILITY

To be coachable, we need humility.

Fred was an excellent basketball player, and he would want you to know that. As a freshman he was moved up to Junior Varsity and earned MVP. At the awards banquet he bragged about his season and cited some of his highlights. He grabbed his trophy, bowed, and walked back to his table to the sound of polite, but weak, applause.

When he got back to his table, he proudly held up his trophy to his mom, "MVP! How many great men are there in the world today?"

His mother thought for a while and then wisely said, "One less than you think."

Humility is on the endangered species list. There aren't too many obvious role models for humility. Humility, by its own definition, is low-key; it doesn't seek attention. Our culture is more attracted to the proud, trash-talking celebrity or athlete than the genuine servant-type. Yet humility is essential if you want to be coachable.

Have you noticed that pride comes easily? We don't have to work at acquiring pride. We don't need to attend classes like "Pride 101" or "I Am the King of the World" seminars. Pride comes naturally to people.

Pride is the enemy of humility. It is opposes true Christlike character. *"God opposes the proud but gives grace to the humble"* (James 4:6).

In fact, God says He hates pride (see Proverbs 6:16-19).

Pride is the sin of mental contrasts. We compare our strengths with the other guy's weaknesses. We try to make ourselves feel better by putting the other person down. It is easy to pick out the other person's weaknesses and contrast them with our strengths.

Pride is a gateway sin to other sins. Just as we have gateway drugs, such as marijuana, pride is a sin that leads to other harmful sins. It can lead to lying, violence, scheming, evil behavior, gossiping, and conflict (see Proverbs 6:17).

Pride makes us depend on our own strengths. It leaves us to depend on our own experience and perspective. Pride develops an obsessive defense. It will protect itself even at the cost of truth, peace, and health. Untreated pride can be destructive.

To be coachable, we must give up the idea that God needs our talent and us. We must come to Him with humility and dependence. We come to Him on our knees.

> *"Humble yourselves before the Lord, and He will lift you up."*
> (James 4:10)

RESPONSE

1. Who comes to your mind as a good example of being *coachable?*

2. What is the opposite of being *coachable?* Give some examples.

3. What is the difference between *training* and *teaching?* How do *you* like to learn?

4. The definition of mentoring is *connecting youth with adults from whom they can learn and receive coaching, encouragement, and guidance.* Discuss each of the key words in this definition.

5. Why do you think pride can be a *gateway sin to other sins?*

A LETTER TO MY SON

Dear Son,

Choosing to be *coachable* can be difficult for us guys. We do pride naturally; it comes with the territory. Arrogance is applauded by our culture. Humility is often viewed as a sign of weakness. Humility is the first step toward maturing and learning.

Humility is the gateway to all other godly character traits. Just as pride is the gateway sin, humility makes it possible for other qualities and skills to emerge.

Why?

Because we aren't pretending that we know it all. We are willing to be trained.

Humility isn't simply good for us; it's good for our relationships. When we are humble before God it will affect how we relate to Him and all other relationships. When we are aware of our sinful and puny selves before a holy and almighty God, we will not self-righteously compare ourselves to others. We will not get caught up in the small stuff. We can be humble in our relationships with other people because we have humbled ourselves before our Heavenly Father. This is critical: *We cannot experience humility in any other relationship until we experience real humility before God.*

How do we develop humility?

Practice. It's like anything else in life. You will struggle at first, but as you work at it, you will get better. Try practicing these three qualities to develop humility in your life:

1. *Coachable.* Be open to training and improving your skills.

2. *Honor others.* Place others above your own concerns, needs, and position. A humble man demonstrates honor to others by considering their interests above his own.

3. *Serve others.* In God's economy, to be great you must serve (see John 13:15-17). Serving means to meet the needs of the other person. True greatness does not depend on what you have, how popular you are, or how talented you are. True greatness in God's eyes is serving each other.

One of the world's most obnoxious sights is someone who is stuck on himself and who has no clue. Pride is so obvious to everyone else except the proud person.

Son, I hope you can avoid the sneaky and destructive ways of pride. Pride is disgusting. Humility is attractive.

Love,
Dad

JOURNAL

Respond to the letter by writing your own thoughts in the section below. Parents may want to use Tim's letter as a model for their own.

_____

_____

_____

_____

_____

_____

_____

_____

_____

▶ CONNECTION ◀

Coachability Lessons

Train to be coachable. Choose two of the following seven suggestions to help you be coachable, honor others, and serve them:

1. Let someone else choose the next movie, video, or restaurant.

2. Ask someone to pray with you and for you.

3. Tour a museum.

4. Ask about your parent or teen's hobby; then listen.

5. Quietly, without anyone knowing, complete the most disgusting chore at your house.

6. Keep a prayer list for your family and friends. Keep it current. Ask them for their requests.

7. Write a letter of appreciation to someone who has helped you.

CHAPTER 3

FROM MAMA TO MENTOR

What would you think about a freshman in high school who has his mom lay out his clothes for him before he got dressed for school? What would you think about this ninth grader if he had his mom come to soccer practice with a first-aid kit and a blanket, "Just in case he got an 'owie'"?

You would think this kid has a problem. "He needs to grow up," you might say.

As children and teens, we need to grow up. The same is true of our parents. In my parenting seminar, The Relaxed Parent, I like to remind parents that they need to grow up with their kids. Some stare at me kind of funny. Others look as if they are getting mad. "You need to change your parenting stance from one of control to one of influence. Give up on the notion of control. You can control your child when he or she is age three. 'Pick up the toys or you won't get to play with them later.'"

Control works when kids are younger, but it doesn't work when they get older, like right now. Your parents can't control you when you are at school or over at a friend's. They don't know what you are doing or what you are up to. That is why I tell parents, "Give up on trying to control your preteen or teen. Seek to influence him instead."

BART'S DAD

Bart's dad tried to control him. Even though Bart was fourteen, his dad tried to make choices for him. It made him mad. Bart's dad didn't like Bart's haircut, so he told him. He didn't like the kind of clothes he wore. He complained, "Those pants are so baggy they would fit a hippo!" Bart's dad didn't like his friends, so he tried to keep Bart away from them. It didn't work. All it did was make Bart angrier with his dad and sneakier about his activities and friends.

Bart's dad was focusing on the externals. He didn't take time to understand how Bart felt and what he was thinking. Since he didn't know his own son, he didn't trust him. He tried to parent him the same way he did when Bart was eight years old. It wasn't effective.

As our children mature, *parents need to help them do more as they do less.* Parents should help prepare kids to make wise decisions on their own. This means kids need to show their parents that they are *ready* to make decisions on their own. If you want to help your mom or dad move from trying to control you, then show her or him you are ready for the next level.

I like to think of this next level as Coaching. The first level of parenting could be called Protecting. When a child is an infant until age three, a parent spends a lot of time just trying to keep the kid alive! The next level could be called Directing. This lasts from ages three to about nine or ten. This is the time a parent teaches values and seeks to build *Impression Points* into children's lives. When a child reaches ten or eleven, this is the time to start the transition to the Coaching level. Instead of telling a child what to do and trying to control his behavior, a parent watches the behavior and gives instruction or correction—like a coach does.

This seems to work well at this stage of development, because kids are already trying to become their own selves, separate from their parents. We call this process individuation—the process of becoming an individual.

Parents often struggle with this process because it feels like rejection. Kids, try to understand their feelings, and remember that your parents have a lot invested in you. They can get a little uptight because they have spent twelve years or more protecting, directing, loving, and providing for you, and your response is "leave me alone!" It can make for some tension.

Some parents get too busy in their lives and don't take the time to get to know their kids. Instead of really knowing their teens, they treat them like a symbol or a stereotype. "My son, the soccer player." "My son, the artist." This is the least demanding way to deal with teens. Stressed and hurried parents tend to focus only on what they see or the symbol they imagine their child to be.

You can help your parents get past this. Instead of focusing on the externals, like sports, activities, and friends, help them focus on the internals—who you are on the *inside*. Trust me, it will be to your advantage.

That is what this book is all about: *helping parents learn to coach their kids*. It is about teens sharing their thoughts, opinions, and values with their mom or dad. It's about a parent taking time to listen, to observe, and to affirm: "Hey, I never looked at it that way. I can tell you have really been doing some thinking."

Our goal is to develop an inner commitment to building character. We don't want to get sidetracked by the externals; we want to focus on who we are and who we are becoming, from the inside out.

Response

1. What do you think about this idea of parents changing their stance from one of control to one of influence?

2. Why do you think some parents try to control their teenagers?

3. Imagine that you are Bart's dad's friend. What would you say to him?

4. What do you think of a parent becoming like a coach? What are the strengths? What are the weaknesses?

5. Describe a time when you noticed a parent stereotype his or her teenage son or daughter.

A Letter To My Son

Dear Son,

I used to coach high school track and field. As a coach I could get away with telling teenage guys what to do: "Take two laps." "Do the stretch right." "Spend more time warming up." They usually listened to me. That's because I was their coach. We had something in common: we wanted to compete well at track and field.

The athletes listened to me because I knew what I was talking about. I have competed too. I have knowledge and experience they can benefit from.

Sometimes I wonder if they listened and responded to me more than their parents.

What do you think?

A coach shares a common interest with his athlete. Both work hard to perform well and make improvements. The coach points out how to perform better. A coach seeks to improve his technique, knowledge of the sport, and skills. A good parent does the same.

Parents who relate as a coach to their teen will work with him to perform better. They will try to make improvements by helping him learn the fine points of technique. They will seek to instruct and impart wisdom (knowledge of the game of life). And they will help their teen develop skills to use in the game of life: *Life Skills.*

"Listen, my son, to your father's instruction and do not forsake your mother's teaching. They will be a garland to grace your head and a chain to adorn your neck . . . Hold on to instruction, do not let it go; guard it well, for it is your life" (Prov. 1:8-9; 4:13).

Listening to your parent's instruction is like following a winning coach. It will be like a gold medal hanging from your neck with ribbon. Good listening skills demonstrate that you are *coachable,* that you are wise and can take instruction. We can learn a lot from other people's experience. We don't have to experience something ourselves to learn.

I have had experiences (some good, some bad) that I want to share with you. I hope they will help you avoid some of the mistakes I made. To dismiss instruction and not be coachable is foolish. According to Proverbs, we should not only follow instruction, but also guard it, because "it is your life."

Love,
Coach Dad

JOURNAL

Respond to the letter by writing your own thoughts here. Parents may want to use Tim's letter as a model for their own.

_____

_____

_____

_____

_____

_____

_____

_____

_____

➡ CONNECTION ⬅

Read the sports section of the newspaper and see if you can come up with two examples of coaches: a good example and a bad example. Discuss as a parent and teen together.

CHAPTER 4

WHAT MAKES A REAL MAN?

G uys are looking for a challenge, especially a pointless one. When guys enter the testosterone zone, they are prepared to grunt, pose, and do incredibly dumb things. It's all about being macho.

"Surf hasn't been this big in a decade. It must be twenty feet!"

"And look, only about twenty guys out," I observed.

"Are you going out?" asked Mike as he crinkled his forehead.

"Sure, why not? I'll just paddle around the point."

"Hmm. Are you sure?"

"Yeah, let's go."

We donned our wetsuits. We walked past a hundred or more spectators on the beach. Most were awestruck with the power and sheer size of the surf. Video cameras whirred. The motor drives of thirty-five-millimeter cameras filled the salty air with their ratchet sounds.

Wimps! I thought. *These spectators don't have the guts. No guts, no glory!*

We paddled out at Rincon Point that sunny winter day. I wasn't about to miss out on epic surf.

It was a beautiful day to drown.

As soon as I approached the surf, a cleanup set came in. Cleanup sets are called that because they tend to wash the weak, the small, and the scared to the beach. It's great if you are outside when a cleanup set comes, but I was inside. I got pounded. I was almost washed back to the rocks. I desperately paddled through the next smaller set. It was only about eighteen feet. When you are at the bottom of an eighteen-foot wave, you are looking at almost thirty feet of water directly over your head.

I couldn't find Mike. I was all alone.

Why did I do this? What was I trying to prove? Can those people on the beach see me getting tossed like I'm in a washing machine? Will I drown today?

After thirty minutes of paddling, I gave up. I didn't have the right board for huge surf. I needed a "gun," like Mike's. I finally spotted him in the lineup. He took off on a peak and descended into the swirling abyss. He was in perfect position. He must have been smiling.

I, on the other hand, was about to get smashed into the rocks. The tide had come up, and the ten-foot shore break was pounding directly onto the boulders. I had to get out of there or die. I paddled with my last remnant of strength. My arms were burning. My shoulders felt like sandbags. I finally reached a section that was breaking and would carry me down the shore, away from the rocks, and to the safety of the beach. I glanced over my shoulder to see a giant mound of water coming toward me. It was coming fast, picking up speed as it entered the shallow water. I paddled to align myself with the peak. With a few strokes I caught it; then it dropped. As I took off, I saw before me a fifteen-foot drop into about two feet of water. The powerful wave had sucked up all the water.

I have to make this wave or I'll get drilled into the sand!

"Whoa, God! Help me!" I screamed.

He did.

I made the drop, tucked in under the lip, and hung on for life as the wave screamed right over me.

The wave dumped me at the small strand of sand. I stumbled to the beach and fell flat on my face in the sand, exhausted. I don't like sand on my face, but it beats getting it smashed into the boulders.

What a stupid thing! I could have drowned out there. I have no business surfing in this.

DARES

Why do we do this? When a guy gets challenged, chances are he'll do it, even if it is pointless and dangerous. Guys have a built-in device called a "Dare-ometer." It kicks in and warns the guy, "Ready Alert—you have been challenged. Stand by for action!"

The testosterone takes over and all common sense and self-preservation flies out the window. World wars have been started by a couple of guys daring each other.

The challenge may be dangerous, stupid, and even pointless; it doesn't matter. If a guy is challenged, he must respond. It's part of the Guy Code. I think this explains a lot of the cases in hospital emergency rooms.

Guys like to compete. Women like to cooperate. That's why women don't do as many stupid things as guys. They don't have to respond to a challenge. They can simply walk away.

What makes a real man? Is it being macho? Is it winning the challenge? Authentic men have discovered their purpose. God has created us to be fully masculine—not partially masculine.

Where did we get this lame idea that Jesus is a wimp? When a guy meets Jesus, he is encountering God. Jesus is fully God and fully man. As a guy gets to know Jesus, he discovers a real man, a masculine man, one who squarely faces life's challenges, temptations, and problems and conquers them. Jesus was no wimp.

As we get to know Jesus, we discover that He does not take away our manhood, He helps us discover it.

RESPONSE

1. Describe a time when you were dared.

2. Did you go through with it? How did you feel afterward?

3. Why do you think most guys find it difficult to walk away from a challenge?

4. When you think of a real man, who comes to mind? What are the qualities that you like in him?

5. Discuss Jeremiah 17:10. How does this Scripture passage make you feel?

A LETTER TO MY SON

Dear Son,

Warrior. Prince. Knight. Athlete. Sensitive. Caring. Compassionate. Communicative.

What makes a man?

Being a man means different things to different people. Let's jump into the debate. What makes a real man? Is it skill or is it heart?

I believe that genuine masculinity involves every part of a guy. To help you remember, consider the three Hs: Head, Heart, and Hand.

Masculinity begins in your head. "As he thinks within himself, so he is" (Prov. 23:7, NASB).

Our thoughts affect our behavior and our character. Our thinking determines who we are.

If you think that being a man means being a tough, macho jock, then you will act like the guys in a beer commercial. If you think to be a man means charming and seducing women, you will attempt your best "Bond, James Bond," impression. What you imagine a real man to be shapes your expectations of yourself.

Who should determine what these images of masculinity are in your mind? Your coach? Hollywood? Magazines? Your friends?

I believe that the best source for determining true masculinity is the Designer. The One who created male and female in the first place.

God expresses the connection between head, heart, and hand: "I, the LORD search the heart and examine the mind, to reward a man according to his conduct, according to what his deeds deserve" (Jer. 17:10).

God is looking for a man who is pleasing to Him. It works from the inside out. Christ's strongest words were against men who were posers, men who pretended to be strong and holy on the outside, but who were actually weak and disgusting on the inside.

What makes a real man? Control over his head. A real man controls his thoughts; he isn't a slave to them.

But God is also searching for the heart. A real man has his heart set on the right things. His ambitions and desires are honorable.

We have seen many men who have their hearts set on financial success. Their hearts are set on making money. As a result, they have sacrificed important relationships because of their greed. Relationships with their families and God have suffered. A man's heart is rather exclusive, for he can only have a few important things on his heart. Happy is the man who keeps the truly important things as top priorities.

I like this Scripture from Jeremiah because it gives us the balance between the mental, the emotional, and the physical. A real man has a disciplined mind, a courageous heart, and a practical hand. He does something!

We need real men, men with disciplined minds, courageous hearts, and hands of compassion. I want to help you become that kind of man.

Are you interested?

With anticipation,
Dad

JOURNAL

Respond to the letter by writing your own thoughts here. Parents may want to use Tim's letter as a model for their own.

_____

_____

_____

_____

_____

_____

_____

_____

_____

◆ CONNECTION ◆

To help strengthen your relationship, try the following: As a parent-son team, try making a Real Man poster. Get a piece of poster board and draw a line down the middle. On the left, write in large letters REAL MAN; on the right, write POSER. Pull out the sports page and read some articles together. Clip out pictures or articles that fit under each category. For one week, look for more examples to put on your poster.

Watch a movie, a sporting event, or the news to get more examples. Sports magazines and personality magazines (like *People* magazine) are full of them. Clip them out or write them on your poster.

The goal is to visually reinforce the difference between what our culture says makes a real man and what really makes a real man.

CHAPTER 5

FEELINGS AND OTHER DISTRACTIONS

*B*ig boys don't cry.
Real men don't get emotional.
Don't trust your feelings.
Only weak people are emotional.
Do any of these sayings sound familiar?

I grew up with these messages ringing in my head. Several adults told me that I shouldn't cry.

But it feels right to cry, I silently protested.

"Just buck up and be a man!"

But it hurts, and crying makes me feel better.

Feelings are not something guys often talk about, unless we are happy about winning the game or mad about someone trying to steal our girl-friend. Anger is the most commonly accepted emotion for guys to discuss, but what about fear? Worry? Disappointment? Who wants to talk about these feelings?

It's not easy for me to write about feelings. I may be somewhat dis-abled in writing about the topic, since I haven't seen many examples of men sharing their feelings. Why is this so? Are we afraid of our emotions? *If we talk about our feelings, they may overpower us. Feelings are just for women; men do, women feel!*

Are we afraid that if we become too emotional we'll be considered effeminate?

I don't want to get too touchy-feely; people might think I'm a pansy.

What is it about feelings that scare us?

Ever since the Garden of Eden man has challenged the rules. We think we can ignore warnings and do our own thing. Feelings are signs of what is going on inside us. They aren't right or wrong. In other words, it's not morally wrong to feel sad. In fact, the Bible teaches that we can be angry and not sin (see Ephesians 4:26).

Our feelings are like road signs that guide us and warn us. We need to learn to read them and follow their advice. Many guys spend their lives running over these road signs of emotions: Plowing over YIELD. Running the STOP. Speeding up when they encounter CAUTION. Is it any wonder they find themselves lost or totaled on the side of the road?

God made our feelings to alert us. If we tune into them, we can become much more aware. By being aware and alert, we will be ready to take on what life hands us. We will be able to respond rather than react.

It is my theory that guys are often afraid of feelings because feelings are so powerful. We are afraid that they will control us. If we pretend they don't exist, or that we can master them, it gives us a false sense of control.

As guys, we have learned to distrust our feelings. *Feelings are not important.* They are considered second-class citizens. In some circles, feelings are completely discounted. This bothers me. *Did God make a mistake? Did He mess up for a few minutes and mistakenly shape feelings into our design?*

I don't think so.

God made us emotional beings on purpose. Our feelings, positive and negative alike, are part of His design. We are created in His image. We have minds, wills, and hearts. As whole people we have the capacity to feel and express our feelings. This makes us like God. Being emotional doesn't make you less of a man; it might make you more like God.

Because most guys don't understand and know how to express their feelings, they don't know how to deal with emotional pain. To avoid dealing with pain, some guys try to keep really busy with school, work, sports, or hobbies. Others seek to deaden the pain with alcohol or drugs. Instead of running away from our feelings, we need to face them.

LEARNING TO FEEL

If God made us with feelings, we should learn to use them, not avoid them. Here are four ways to learn to trust your feelings. They spell out an acrostic for **F.E.E.L.**

Feelings are designed by God. Being a whole person, created in God's image, means accepting that we will have feelings.

Evaluate your feelings. Ask yourself, *Why do I feel this way? What does this emotion signal? Should I pay attention to something?* Our feelings are like the gauges on our car's dashboard. They help us know how everything is running. They alert us to problems.

Expand your vocabulary to express your feelings. If someone asks you, "How was your day?" Instead of saying, "Okay," try to be more descriptive and add some feeling to it. You might even attempt a word picture to express your true feelings. "I felt like I was getting squeezed by a vise. Everyone wants a piece of me."

Listen to your own feelings and the feelings of others. Look for clues about how they are doing emotionally. Watch the nonverbal cues like posture, facial expressions, tone of voice, and arm position. By tuning into the feelings of others, you will become more skilled in listening to your own feelings.

The shortest verse in the Bible is also one of the most powerful. It demonstrates how God created us with feelings. The verse? John 11:35: "Jesus wept."

RESPONSE

1. What are some sayings similar to *Big boys don't cry?*

2. What do you think about the statement, "Men *do*, women feel."

3. Give an example of how some guys run over the road signs of emotions. Discuss why they do this.

4. Discuss the ways God demonstrates His emotions.

5. What do you think about the statement, "Being emotional doesn't make you less of a man; it might make you more like God?"

A LETTER TO MY SON

Dear Son,

"Jesus wept." The words are haunting. The Creator of the universe. Our Savior. The powerful and everlasting King of kings cried. He wept.

It doesn't fit with our image of heroes.

"Jesus wept." At a time of loss, He demonstrated His true emotions. We don't think less of Him for this; we think more of Him.

It reminds me of Romans 12:15, "When others are happy, be happy with them. If they are sad, share their sorrow" (NLT).

How can we do this without getting emotional? According to this verse, to obey God we must get emotional.

It was on a warm August day that I got a phone call from the emergency room. A three-year-old girl had fallen into a swimming pool, and her life hung in the balance. "Would you come to be with the family?"

"Sure, I'll be there in a few minutes." I wasn't sure what I would say. What do you say to a mother whose child might die? I thought about my theological training. She didn't need a lecture on the sovereignty of God. I thought about my education in psychology. She didn't need to hear about the five stages of grief. I thought about my years of work with children and youth. She didn't need my advice on waterfront supervision. As I walked into the emergency room, I uttered a silent prayer, *Lord, give me the words to help this mom in the midst of this crisis.* This verse popped into my head, "When others are happy, be happy with them. If they are sad, share their sorrow." I decided to not say much. Instead, I hugged the mother, listened to her, and cried with her.

Later, I offered a weepy prayer. I spent the night with the family in the waiting room. We chatted a little and cried a lot. The girl died in the morning. Later, her mother told me it was my tears that ministered to her.

Sometimes, to obey God we must get emotional.

Son, don't be afraid of your emotions. God gave them to you to make you complete. Learn to use your emotions, not to avoid them. They are resources that will help you in life. When we embrace our emotions we begin to have a whole heart. This helps us experience much more of life. When we begin to use our emotions instead of running from them, our lives will have a new energy.

Sometimes, real men cry.

Love,
Dad

JOURNAL

Respond to the letter by writing your own thoughts in the section below. Parents may want to use Tim's letter as a model for their own.

_____

_____

_____

_____

_____

_____

_____

_____

➡ CONNECTION ⬅

As teen and parent, go out and sit in your car. Turn the key on the ignition to the first click. Don't start the car, just turn on the ignition to where the dashboard lights up. Notice how many indicator and warning lights there are. Try to match up a light with a feeling. Examples: Feeling cool when the temperature gauge is on C. Or feeling drained when the gas is on E.

Then go for a drive and see how many different road signs you can find. How are these like our feelings? Example: YIELD could mean you don't always have to have your way.

Top off the drive by going to get some ice cream. Suggestion: Since this has been a road trip, try Rocky Road!

CHAPTER 6

NO FEAR

S CHOOL SHOOTINGS LEAVE 4 DEAD, 12 WOUNDED"
"SHOOTER ATTACKS CHURCH YOUTH RALLY"
"13-YEAR-OLD KILLS PARENTS AND CLASSMATES"
"GANGS INFILTRATE RURAL TOWNS"

The last few years much attention has focused on teen violence. It seems as though you can't even go to school, meet in a prayer group, or attend a youth rally at church without the risk of being shot at. These kinds of shootings were unheard of five years ago, but now they seem commonplace.

What is going on?

Why is our world so violent?

Where can I go to be safe?

I have seen violence creep into our neighborhood as well. Our town is reported to be one of the safest communities in America, yet we have our share of problems too.

It is scary.

In fact, you can be afraid anywhere.

Even in the mountains!

I was backpacking with a group of high school guys in the High Sierras. We backpacked in several miles to Beck Lakes to discover twenty-foot waterfalls coming down from the lake.

"Did you know you could go behind these? It's really cool." I asked.

"Go ahead, Tim. It looks too big," said Steve.

"You'll get crunched," warned Robert.

Five teens watched as their youth pastor and guide dove into the chilling, churning water.

The waterfall was larger than I thought. I had greatly underestimated the volume of the water. The water cascaded from thirty feet, not twenty feet as I guessed. It was thicker and wider than I had anticipated. I had a difficult time swimming through the pounding surge. After several attempts, I made it through.

Behind the falls I discovered a beautiful emerald cavern.

"COME ON IN! IT'S GREAT IN HERE!" I shouted. I could see five blurry figures staring into the waterfall.

They could not hear me.

I swam over to the mossy wall to find a ledge to rest on. The chill from the runoff of melting snow made me breathe fast and tire quickly.

To my horror, I found no ledge. With anxiety mounting, I swam frantically around the crashing chamber to find only mossy vertical walls. I had been treading for five or ten minutes, and I was fatiguing quickly.

I have to find a shallow spot where I can stand.

I dove under the water in search of a rock, a branch, or a foothold to stand on. I dove again.

Again.

Again.

The entire cavern was fifteen feet deep. No place to rest.

I will have to swim out before I drown.

I pushed off the slimy wall and swam under water at about six feet down. The turbulence from the falls thrust me back into the cavern. I tried again at eight feet.

Then at ten.

Twelve.

Fifteen.

I can't get out of this slimy, freezing pit! Again I tried pulling myself along the bottom at fifteen feet down, but the backwash from the falls kept pushing me back. I yelled at the guys at the top of my chilled lungs, "HELP ME! I CAN'T GET OUT!"

But they couldn't hear me. They just stood there staring right at me, shifting their weight, squinting their eyes, trying to catch a glimpse of me in the dark cavern.

Then I remembered God. In my terror I had forgotten Him.

"God, help me survive. Rescue me from this water!"

I heard God whisper to me, "Give it up. I'll take care of you."

Give it up? What does He mean?

Then it occurred to me: *I had tried everything in my own strength, now I needed to surrender to God.*

I knew what I needed to do. I took a deep breath and swam with all my strength toward the deafening falls. As the current hit me, I gave into it and let it pull me down. It slammed me into the bottom and I let out all the air in my lungs.

I prayed, *I'm giving it up to You, God. I am in Your hands.*

The turbulent current tossed me around as if I was inside a dryer at the Laundromat. After a few minutes of being pummeled by the pounding force of the water, I passed out.

I drifted into some underwater current, which eventually took me past the eddy of the waterfall, downstream, and to the surface. My back-packing buddies pulled me from the water and laid me on a rock.

They thought I was dead.

The waterfall was scary. But what was really scary was Steve attempting mouth-to-mouth resuscitation. I came to just as his lips were inches away!

In spite of my foolishness, I learned a huge lesson. "When you pass through the waters, I will be with you; and when you pass through the rivers, they will not sweep over you. When you walk through the fire, you will not be burned" (Isa. 43:2).

I learned that God is with us when we are in deep waters (or when we are in deep yogurt).

I learned that *security is not in a place, but it is in a person.* Wherever we go in life there will be waters, rivers, and fires. But we don't walk alone. God is with us. He is our source of protection. He is our refuge and strength.

"God is our refuge and strength, an ever-present help in trouble. There-fore we will not fear, though the earth give way and the mountains fall into the heart of the sea . . . the Lord Almighty is with us" (Ps. 46:1-2, 7).

RESPONSE

1. Describe where you feel safe. Where do you feel the least safe?

2. How does God (who is spirit) help us with things that are scary and physical (like tornadoes, earthquakes, fires, and deep water)?

3. Share a story (it doesn't have to be an adventure) about a time when you were afraid.

4. Read Isaiah 43:2 again. What are some waters, rivers, and fires we encounter in life?

5. Discuss: *Security is not in a place, but it is in a person.*

A LETTER TO MY SON

Dear Son,

You are sure to encounter challenges that will make you feel as though you are drowning in deep waters. It is my experience that the safest place to be is in God's hands. I wish I could always be there to help you, rescue you, or protect you. But I know I can't.

God can. He is always available, strong, and loving. He is our refuge and strength. We can be afraid in the mountains, at school, or on the streets. The place doesn't matter. Fear can strike anywhere. Fear can strike anyone.

But as 2 Timothy 1:7 reminds us, "God did not give us a spirit of timidity, but a spirit of power, of love and of self-discipline." With God's help, we can face our fears. There will be times when we need His power. Maybe we will need His power to stand up for what is right. There will be times when we need His love. You might have to do a school project with someone you can't stand. You need God's love to do it. And there are other times when you will need self-discipline to face your fears. I see these as a balance: on one end you have power, on the other end you have love, and in the middle you have self-discipline. Self-discipline gives you the flexibility to move from power to love and back.

If we have God's Spirit influencing us, we have the balance and self-control to respond in a way we need to. We don't have to react. We don't have to be defensive or try to control someone. We can respond instead of react.

I have observed that when we are prepared for situations, we aren't afraid of them. Following this verse helps us prepare with Spirit preparation.

Remember, God doesn't promise to deliver you from the waters, rivers, and fires of life; but He does promise to be with you in the middle of them!

In His grip,
Dad

Journal

Respond to the letter by writing your own thoughts here. Parents may want to use Tim's letter as a model for their own.

_____

_____

_____

_____

_____

_____

_____

_____

➡ Connection ⬅

If you have access to the Internet, do a search on "teen violence" and "school shootings." Discuss, as teen and parent, what you find. Develop a plan on what to do if there was a shooting or bomb threat at your work or school.

CHAPTER 7

THE MAN IN
THE MIRROR

The baseball coach squinted his eyes and asked me, "Ever play before, Smith?"

"Yeah," I lied, "all the time."

"What position?"

"Umm . . . usually outfield."

"What field?"

"*Out* field!"

"Left, center, or right?" he asked impatiently.

I caught the last word he said and repeated it, "Right."

"Get out there and show us your stuff!"

I ran to get my glove. *Right field. Right field. Is that behind third base? Must be, because that would be right as you face home plate.* I jogged out between shortstop and third base.

"Smith! That's *left* field! I said *right* field!" He pointed between first and second.

Everyone laughed. I felt smaller than the grass I was running on. I thought I was a baseball player. I had my glove, my cap, my spikes, my cool looking pants, and my baseball socks, but I wasn't a baseball player. At age ten I was already a failure at Little League, and I hadn't even played a game. In fact, I hadn't even started my first practice, and I felt like a loser.

That is the problem when we play the comparison game. Whenever we compare ourselves to others, we will always lose. There will always be people who are bigger, faster, smarter, richer, better looking, more talented, and more popular.

Feeling negative about who we are affects all of our lives. It impacts our self-image (that is, how we think about ourselves), as well as our identity (who we consider ourselves to be, different and distinct from others).

A common phrase in our culture is, "Take a look at the man in the mirror." That means taking a close look at yourself. The Bible encourages us to do this:

> Do not merely listen to the word, and so deceive yourselves. Do what it says. Anyone who listens to the word but does not do what it says is like a man who looks at his face in a mirror and, after looking at himself, goes away and immediately forgets what he looks like. But the man who looks intently into the perfect law that gives freedom, and continues to do this, not forgetting what he has heard, but doing it—he will be blessed in what he does (James 1:22-25).

If we look at ourselves in the reflection of the mirror of God's Word, we get an accurate reflection of ourselves.

Aren't you glad you have a mirror? Can you imagine someone getting up in the morning and seeing morning hair, spinich lodged in teeth, sleep encrusted eyes, and then ignoring all that he has seen and going to school?

Disgusting, huh?

When we look into the mirror we notice some good things and some bad things. Normally we leave the good alone and spend some time on the bad.

The Bible helps us focus on who God says we are. It helps us pay attention to some of the things that need attention. Listening to what God has to say about who we are is always going to be more accurate and helpful than listening to what people say. People get hung up on the externals. God cuts right through to what is on the inside. (Read 1 Samuel 16:7.)

When we focus on the externals, we actually set ourselves up for more pressure. We strive to be something we aren't. Trying to discover our identity by working on the outside forces us to be superficial or fake.

LITTLE LEAGUE FATIGUE

My starting year in Little League was also my retiring year. Through many strikeouts, dropped balls, errors, and general poor play, I began to doubt that I was a baseball player.

It was the last of the season and we were tired of Coach yelling. But of course, he did. "Fielders, get out there and catch some flies!"

I was dead tired, thirsty, and melting in the ninety-degree heat. Now I had to look up into the scorching sun and catch a stupid, white ball. I wasn't enjoying this game at all. *How can it be "America's Pastime?" I think I will defect to Russia and play chess.*

"Crack!" went the bat. The ball flew high. I lost it in the sun. I kept staring, hoping to see it. I never saw it, but I *felt* it.

"Whamm!" it smacked me on the back of my head. I fell to the grass. It knocked me out cold.

When I came to, Coach asked, "Are you okay, Smith? You know you should keep your eye on the ball."

With my head throbbing, and trying to focus on the two blurry coaches before me, I shouted, "I quit!" I walked home.

That day I learned a powerful insight about myself: I am not a baseball player.

RESPONSE

1. Describe a humiliating sports experience.

2. What are some ways we play the Comparison Game?

3. What is tragic about a man who "listens to the word, but does not do what it says"?

4. Why is God's evaluation of us more accurate than others' evaluation?

5. Why is it important to know who you are not?

A LETTER TO MY SON

Dear Son,

Taking a good look at yourself will help you in life. How so? If you can decide who you are, it will give you the freedom to be that person. It will reduce the pressure to perform. You may not be able to control all the externals. But you will know who you are from the inside out. You will be able to influence the situation if you know who you are. You may not be able to control the externals, but you can do something about the internals.

You can't always control what is happening to you, but you can control your response to it.

Son, the first step in discovering who you are is deciding who you aren't. It may not be real clear who you are; your identity may still be fuzzy. But start by deciding who you definitively are not.

That is what John the Baptist did. You know, the hairy guy in the Bible who wore animal skins, ate locusts, and hung out in the desert? His mission: to prepare people to listen to Jesus. It was a challenging job. People were confused.

"You must be the Messiah. Are you the Christ?" asked the religious folk.

"I am not the Christ," responded John.

"Oh, you must be Elijah."

"I am not."

"Then who are you? Are you a prophet?"

"I am the voice of one calling in the desert. 'Make straight the way for the Lord.'"

John could have confused his identity. He could have made himself bigger than he needed to be: "I am the set-up guy for the King of kings. I am His right-hand man, you know. I can put you in touch with the Messiah. Maybe set up a meet?"

John could have made his identity and mission smaller than it needed to be: "Well, I'm nothing but a hairy guy who eats locusts. I am just a bit actor in the greatest drama ever, featuring Jesus, God's Son."

John did neither of these. He didn't confuse his story and identity with Christ's. He didn't let comparison ruin his chance to fulfill his mission. He humbly, simply, told people who he was. He could be himself. (See John 1:19-30.)

John knew who he was. He also knew who he wasn't. His mission was focused because he was clear about his identity.

You don't have to pretend you are something you aren't, and you don't have to pretend you are nothing. Just be yourself.

Son, having a clear picture of who God made you will give you a sense of power in your life. It will set you free to be the man God created you to be. You will be distinct. You will be different. You don't have to be weird. But you will discover that you are custom made.

We can see four qualities of a godly man's identity by looking at the example of John the Baptist. A godly man's identity:

▶ provides purpose,
▶ is based on truth,
▶ lasts forever,
▶ provides him with power.

I believe that *we really don't know ourselves until we find ourselves in Christ*. In Him, we discover ourselves and the power to take on life. "I can do everything through Him who gives me strength" (Phil. 4:13).

Son, take time to look into the mirror of God's Word. Then you will discover who you truly are: a son of God. You'll see a young man with a purpose, who lives by the truth, empowered by God with an eye toward eternity.

Looking with you,
Dad

JOURNAL

Respond to the letter by writing your own thoughts in the section below. Parents may want to use Tim's letter as a model for their own.

_____

_____

_____

_____

_____

_____

_____

_____

_____

_____

◆ CONNECTION ◆

As teen and parent, read James 1:22-25. Talk about how a mirror helps us. Discuss: "How is God's Word like a mirror?" Then make a Man In the Mirror project. Option 1: Purchase two small mirrors with frames, and on them write either a Scripture verse or qualities you aspire to. Use a metallic paint pen or a permanent marker.

Option 2: On a mirror, use a grease pencil to temporarily record qualities you want to develop in your life.

Place your mirror in a prominent spot where it will remind you of the kind of man you want to be.

CHAPTER 8

MVP

wanted to find out what teens thought were their worst "I hate it when that happens" experiences. I asked the kids in our youth group, and here is what they said:

TOP TEN CONFIDENCE KILLERS

"I hate it when . . ."

10. You find out at the end of the day that you have bad breath.
9. You read the list for the team three times and still don't find your name on it.
8. You are polishing your car for a big date and notice in the reflection that you have a giant red zit on your nose.
7. Your "close friend" forgets your name when he is introducing you to a cute girl.
6. You get to camp, excited about a week of fun, only to discover that you forgot your deodorant, underwear, and toothbrush.
5. You forget your locker combination.
4. You lose a school election.
3. You drop your tray in the cafeteria and the food splatters on the most popular couple in school.
2. You throw up at an all-school assembly.
1. You wet the bed, and wake up to discover you are spending the night at your friend's house.

Oh! Aren't those horrendous?

How can we deal with feeling good about ourselves when stuff like that happens?

First, we need to be careful whom we listen to. Listening to the crowd's evaluation of us could be devastating. A better way to discover who you are and feel good about it is to get an accurate reflection of yourself, not simply a drive-by check-out.

What would you say is a true measure of worth? Fame, fortune, reputation, athletic skills, strength, GPA, or good looks? Not everyone can be an MVP (Most Valuable Player), so what makes you valuable?

Some days it is difficult to feel good about yourself. This isn't just during your teenage years. It continues in life. Discouraging, huh?

But it's true. We don't always feel so good about ourselves, whether we are fourteen or forty.

On the road to feeling good about ourselves, there are three pits that we can easily fall into if we don't look out for them. These pits could be called *enemies of self-worth*.

BODY

The first pit is an overemphasis on your *body*. Our culture puts great importance on having the perfect body. Looking good has become a popular national pastime. If you can't look good naturally, look good synthetically: try cosmetic surgery, fake-'n-bake tan, bleached hair, and steroid-enhanced muscles.

I recently read about a sixteen-year-old girl who wanted liposuction and breast enlargement so she would look good for the prom.

Guys can easily get carried away too. I know of some guys who spend more time lifting weights than they do on their homework. They want to have big muscles to show off during their six years of high school.

God doesn't make physical appearance and strength a top priority. Our culture, however, thinks they are important, and we often make foolish decisions based on looking only at the externals.

Do not consider his appearance or his height, for I have rejected him. The Lord does not look at the things man looks at. Man looks at the outward appearance, but the Lord looks at the heart (1 Sam. 16:7).

BRAINS

The second pit that we can fall into on the road to self-worth involves our brains. By this I mean too much emphasis on being smart in order to be valuable. We have the false notion that intelligence equals worth. But in reality, if you act too smart, people won't like you. If you act too dumb, people will look down on you.

There is a lot of pressure in our culture for students to make good grades.

Why?

So that they can get into a good college.

Why?

So that they can get a good job.

Why?

So that they can make a lot of money.

So that is what makes intelligence important? Money?

It is a myth, and a dangerous one at that, that smarter people are more valuable. What determines "smarts"? An IQ test? The grades you get in school?

How you feel about your intelligence could be inaccurate. You could be a lot smarter than you think. Or you may not be as smart as you think. Some tests aren't very good at predicting intelligence or success.

Albert Einstein couldn't read until he was seven years old; later he failed math. What would have happened if his junior high school administrator looked at his scores and didn't let him enroll?

Thomas Edison failed many subjects. His teacher said he would never learn anything.

A newspaper editor fired Walt Disney because "he didn't have any creative ideas."

Wouldn't you hate to be Edison's teacher or Disney's editor twenty years later?

God's view of "smarts" is different from the world's.

> This is what the LORD says: "Let not the wise man boast of his wisdom or the strong man boast of his strength or the rich man boast of his riches, but let him who boasts boast about this: that he understands and knows me, that I am the LORD, who exercises kindness, justice and righteousness on earth, for in these I delight," declares the Lord (Jer. 9:23-24).

BUCKS

Let not the rich man boast of his riches.

The third trap we fall into on the road to self-worth is a false hope in bucks. Wealth can easily become something that defines us. We even use it to describe people by saying things like, "His worth is 1.6 million." We find ourselves paying attention to the person with the most money. Money and its pursuit can be a false hope. It is not wrong to be wealthy, but chasing after riches sidetracks us from following God.

According to God's Word from Jeremiah, our confidence should not be in our financial (or physical) strength, but in our relationship with the Lord.

What does God say to boast (feel positive) about?

Not man's wisdom (brains).

Not strength (body/beauty).

Not wealth (bucks).

But, from God's point of view, biblical self-worth comes from:

1. Knowing and understanding God.
2. Experiencing God's kindness (His grace).
3. Experiencing God's justice (His forgiveness).
4. Growing in righteousness (doing the right thing).
5. Knowing that these are things that delight God.

Bottom line? Forget *Body, Brains,* and *Bucks* and pursue the things that will last. They will give you security and a sense of self-worth that will endure.

RESPONSE

1. What would you add to the Top Ten Confidence Killers?
2. What is *your* true measure of self-worth?
3. How does our culture emphasize Body? Brains? Bucks?
4. Why is it important to know that God looks at the heart?
5. How can we delight in the things God does? (See Jeremiah 9:23-24.)

A LETTER TO MY SON

Dear Son,

My goal in writing you these letters is to help you grow to like yourself, have confidence, and make wise decisions. On the way, you will encounter all kinds of interruptions and detours. We have discussed three pits that could easily sidetrack or ruin you. We can remember guys who have lost it because they became too concerned with their bodies. We don't have to look too far to see guys who have placed all their confidence in their mental abilities. Their brains became their god. And we can easily cite guys who have made money an idol. Bucks are all they live for.

Each one of these can become a false idol: body, brains, or bucks. They promise something they can't deliver. They entice you to place your confidence in them. But each can be as elusive as the morning fog. We need to have our confidence in something that will remain, something solid and dependable.

What it comes down to, son, is *are you more concerned what* they *think,* or *what* He *thinks?* If you are influenced by people's opinion of you, you will chase after body, brains, and bucks. But if you are interested in what God thinks of you, you will chase after what delights Him.

God is more concerned with your character than your reputation.

We will always struggle with self-worth if our goal is to be liked, but we will come to value and accept ourselves as we see ourselves becoming more like Christ.

I delight in you,
Dad

JOURNAL

Respond to the letter by writing your own thoughts in the section below. Parents may want to use Tim's letter as a model for their own.

_____

_____

_____

_____

_____

_____

_____

_____

_____

➡ CONNECTION ⬅

Option A: Rent the film *Rudy* about an undersized, but highly motivated, college football player. Discuss what helped Rudy and what obstacles he faced.

Option B: Watch *Forrest Gump* and discuss his obstacles and his inner strength.

CHAPTER 9

WHERE DO I FIT?

Once upon a time, I was interviewing at a church for the job of youth pastor. I was trying to look cool. I wanted to be liked and to belong. I wanted to fit in.

I slipped into the junior high Sunday School class. I was late because I had been speaking to the high school students, and it had taken longer than planned. My talk had gone fairly well; they laughed at my jokes and seemed to approve of how I looked and was dressed. *So far, so good. This interviewing isn't so tough.*

I stood by the door. A tall guy with a huge moustache introduced me to the class. I walked to the front and began speaking. I talked about what I like to do in youth ministry and a little about myself.

They seemed to like me. *Maybe I will fit in?*

I wanted the job. I wanted the kids and the adults to accept me. I wanted to belong.

After a few minutes of my "commercial," I sat down and people smiled at me—even the goof-offs in the back row!

I knew I had won them. I must have come across as cool, relaxed, understanding, and hip. *Yeah, I was cool, I would fit in.*

After a few minutes of listening to the lesson, I glanced at my watch and panicked. *I was supposed to be in the college class five minutes ago!*

Determined to not get stressed, I reassured myself. *It will be okay; just quietly get up and slip out that door and get down to the college class. Five minutes is no big deal!* I turned and faced a few students nearby. I gave them a cool-guy good-bye nod and subtle wave. I quickly opened the door and shut it behind me.

In my determination to not disturb the class and to move quickly, I had made a mistake. I had stepped into a closet!

There I stood, inside a dark, four-foot-square closet. I felt like a complete idiot! *Now they will think I'm a geek!* My hands fumbled toward the string that was hanging in my face. I pulled the string and a light went on. The bulb, only inches from my face blasted my eyes with blinding brilliance. When my eyes focused, I noticed shelves full of Bibles and Sunday School supplies. I found the doorknob and thrust open the door. Dozens of stunned faces greeted me.

"I meant to do that!" I proclaimed. "Nice supplies." I dashed out of there, this time using the right door. As I left, I glanced over my shoulder at a room full of junior high students laughing their heads off. I felt like a total jerk.

The funny thing is, I got the job!

Later on, some kids told me, "I can just see myself doing something like that."

"When you walked into the closet, we knew you would fit in with us. We are always doing goofy stuff like that. You belong with us!"

"Ah, thanks," I said.

What does it mean to belong? Some of those junior high students, who laughed at my closet charade, became my friends over the years. We have shared many experiences together, some funny, some sad.

Many people seem lonely these days. Maybe it is because a lot of people are looking out for themselves. The average teen feels alone and lonely, even in the midst of the crowd. Wouldn't you like a place where you could belong?

We all need to feel like we fit in—that we belong and have a sense of community. We want to sense that we are connected to others. We hunger to be known and to know others. We want to fit in.

ENEMIES OF FRIENDSHIPS

Why don't we experience more of a sense of belonging? I think it could be due to the things that keep us apart: the enemies of friendships.

One of the enemies of friendships is *individualism,* the pursuit of promoting the individual. It's seen in a "What's-in-it-for-me" mentality. We have done a thorough job in our schools and society of affirming the individual, but we haven't done as good a job in affirming community. We have worked hard at making each person feel special and unique. But the result has been people who focus on themselves instead of working to reach out and to connect with others.

Fear of commitment is the second enemy of friendships. Many teens are afraid of the work and time it takes to really get to know someone and be devoted to something together. Maybe it's because commitment has become a dirty word. For some, commitment was what Dad and Mom had before their divorce. If pain and loss are the result of commitment, forget it!

Unrealistic expectations are the third enemy of friendships. Sometimes we set ourselves up for tragic falls because we have expectations for others which are impossible. We look to others to complete us. "If I could only be with her, then my life would be fulfilled." Looking to others to complete what is lacking in us is an unrealistic hope.

The busy pace of life is the fourth enemy of friendships. Who has time to build friendships? Life is much more transient in this new millennium. People move more than they used to. Teens keep busy with school, sports, activities, jobs, and lessons. Our lives are hurried and without connection. A frantic pace has led us to feel cut off from contact, left unwanted and unknown. We certainly notice the space between relationships. Many people seem distant and guarded. The rush seems to affect our closeness to God as well.

Could we be a culture without friends?

RESPONSE

1. Describe an embarrassing moment.

2. Do you agree or disagree with this statement: "Most people seem lonely these days."

3. Which of the four enemies of friendships have you noticed? Describe.

4. How can we slow down the pace of our lives and connect more with people?

5. What do you like in a friend?

A LETTER TO MY SON

Dear Son,

"Where do I fit in?" is a common question. Most of us are looking for a place to be and people to belong to. That is the beauty of being a Christian. It gives us a place and a people. The place is in the body of Christ. The people are our brothers and sisters in Christ. As Christians, we can demonstrate to others our identity and belonging.

> I appeal to you, brothers, in the name of our Lord Jesus Christ, that all of you agree with one another so that there may be no divisions among you and that you may be perfectly united in mind and thought (1 Cor. 1:10).

A community is a group of people who are one with each other. They aren't clones of each other. Each person has his or her own identity and uniqueness, but each is united under one Lord. This means they have made Christ "boss" of their lives. We aren't our own individual bosses; we all submit to Him. By submitting to one boss, we learn submission and teamwork.

I know you like basketball. Can you imagine a basketball team that doesn't want to submit to the coach? What would happen if every player wanted to do his own thing? It might have five excellent players, but until they learn to submit to their coach and work on their teamwork, they will be a mediocre team.

The same is true of the Christian team. As we submit to our coach—Jesus Christ—then we will have a team that can be one with each other and play well together.

To develop community, each individual needs to give up a little to create unity. He has to give up doing things his way. He has to give up some of who he is to create a team identity. He might have to give up what he desires in order to do whatever helps the team. Part of being a successful team is helping the others.

The same is true about being a successful friend.

Your friend,
Dad

JOURNAL

Respond to the letter by writing your own thoughts in the section below. Parents may want to use Tim's letter as a model for their own.

_____

_____

_____

_____

_____

_____

_____

_____

➡ CONNECTION ◀

Read this chapter again and see if you can come up with a short slogan that summarizes a key concept for you and your parent. Then take a trip to a thrift store to purchase an old trophy; any kind will do. Have fun! Then go to a trophy shop and have a new plate made with your slogan engraved. Pull off the old name plate and stick on the new one. You have created a keepsake to honor your parent-teen friendship.

A sample slogan, for example, might be: United in mind and heart.

CHAPTER 10

HOLA JOEY!

I will never forget how Mexico changed Joey. All I knew about him was that he was the tall, withdrawn kid who rarely came to our youth group. But when it came time to train for our Easter Mexico Mission, he came alive!

I was stunned. Normally, Joey was so timid, he would be afraid to lead out in silent prayer!

I gave him a ride home one Sunday after the training and ventured this question: "Joey, I need a strong guy to help with the set-up team. It is dirty work with a lot of sweat, frustration, and tension. You have to go down early and set up the camp. Your job is to have all of the problems fixed, so that when we get there with the rest of the team, everything works. Are you interested?"

"Yeah, count me in. Do you need help getting the equipment?"

I couldn't believe my ears. My biggest frustration with our annual trip had been obtaining and organizing the equipment. *What a relief to have someone offer to help!* "Sure. Do you have time?"

"What else would I do?"

"Don't you have homework or something else around here?" I gestured to his house as we sat parked in his driveway.

"Nope. My mom is never home. I don't do homework, and I really don't have that much to do around here."

Joey offered to organize the equipment. He even offered to get some new stuff on his own. "Leave it to me. It will be ready."

I had never left a responsibility this large in the hands of a sixteen year old.

When we arrived in Mexico, our camp was perfect. Joey and his set-up team had done an excellent job. The generator was running. The tents were neatly pitched. We had plenty of light and water. Everything was in order. Even the set-up team looked relaxed and clean!

When we began work in our village, Joey instantly became a hero to the Mexican boys. He played volleyball and soccer with them. After lunch, he wrestled with them, gave them piggyback rides, teased them and bought them sodas. He did all of this using the three words of Spanish he knew: *hola* (hello), *adios* (good-bye), and *andale* (run). Joey didn't need Spanish; he had learned the language of love.

At the end of the day, Joey would collapse into his lawn chair, looking completely drained. I have never seen anyone so tired and yet so alive at the same time. Mexico changed Joey.

What happened to Joey? What changed him so radically? Before Mexico, he had no real purpose to his life. No one really needed him to do anything. His mom was divorced and kept busy at work. Joey had no brothers or sisters. He would spend hours at home alone.

Joey came alive in Mexico because he discovered purpose in what he was doing. He realized that maybe for the first time in his life he was making a difference. For the first time in sixteen years, he was doing something meaningful.

Response

1. Why do you think Joey changed in Mexico?
2. Why does service often lead to joy?
3. What kinds of service have you done? How did it make you feel?
4. What is it like serving the needs of someone from another culture?
5. How important is it to you to make a difference with your life? What would you be willing to sacrifice?

A Letter To My Son

Dear Son,

In the rush of our culture, many of us live lives of quiet desperation. Our lives don't seem to count that much. So we hurry to do more in order to feel significant. But we end up only adding to the list, quickening the pace and multiplying our emptiness.

Joey discovered fulfillment for his emptiness. It wasn't *getting* something; it was in *giving* that he discovered something meaningful. He found real meaning in serving others. It made him feel worthwhile. It made him feel significant and part of a team that was making a difference.

It is so easy to get wrapped up in thinking *What's in it for me?* Or *Will my needs be met?* As a result of this type of thinking, we trap ourselves in "react mode." We end up reacting rather than acting. A person who is always reacting becomes a victim of the circumstances that surround him. A person who chooses to act—to take the initiative and serve—can actually influence his environment.

Joey did!

Jesus talks about finding ourselves as we invest ourselves in serving others: "For whoever wants to save his life will lose it, but whoever loses his life for me will find it" (Matt. 16:25).

If we are trying to discover purpose in life by grabbing at it, we will miss it. We shouldn't live our lives as though we are in a beer commercial: "You only go around once in life, so you gotta grab all the gusto you can!" That may work for beer drinking, but it doesn't work for living! The irony is that we find ourselves by losing ourselves.

Son, it is my prayer that you will discover who God made you to be. You are more likely to discover who you are if you are serving.

Joey discovered that he could be compassionate, be caring, and also communicate by losing himself in ministry to the poor children of Mexico. It was in service that he discovered a purpose for his life. It was as if he had been watching TV in black and white for sixteen years, and someone came along and pushed a button on the TV. Instantly, he had color and stereo!

A life with purpose makes a difference.

Viva con Dios!
Dad

JOURNAL

Respond to the letter by writing your own thoughts in the section below. Parents may want to use Tim's letter as a model for their own.

_____

_____

_____

_____

_____

_____

_____

_____

_____

➡ CONNECTION ⬅

Plan a service project that you can do as a parent and teen. If you want, get together with another parent-teen team.

Ideas:

1. Call the local rescue mission and ask what you could do on a Saturday morning.

2. Contact your local Crisis Pregnancy Center to see if it needs help.

3. What is a forgotten and needy group in your area? Do some research to find out what it needs, then develop a plan to help.

4. Ask a nursery for a donation of plants that aren't selling. Get some potting soil and some kind of unique container (from your garage or a thrift store), pot the plants, and offer them to seniors in a retirement or convalescent home.

CHAPTER 11

SEAN'S DISCOVERY

H ey Sean! How was Grad Night?" Sean and his girlfriend, Jennifer, were lining up to march into the stadium at their high school graduation. I came to see them and congratulate them.

"Oh, it was fun. We had a blast." He pulled Jen in close.

"Hi Jen. Congratulations."

A huge smile spread across her face, revealing her perfect teeth. "Thanks. Yeah, last night was fun." She then looked toward the stadium filled with people.

"Are you nervous?"

"Yes, I am. There are so many people here."

"There are so many people graduating. Look at this line. It stretches all the way to the end of the driveway!"

"Yeah, it's one of the largest graduating classes," Sean said proudly. The kelly green gown brought out the green in his eyes. In them I could see anticipation.

"I believe it. Are you happy to be done?" I asked.

"What a relief!" Sean admitted.

"I am looking for a break before college," Jen said as she raised her eyebrows.

"Yeah, give your brains a break this summer. I hope to see you at college group. Congratulations. I'll take some photos." I shook their hands and joined the throng in the stands.

That summer, Sean and Jen became regulars at our college summer Bible study. We held it in our backyard. We had so many students come that we didn't fit into our living room. So we spread some blankets on the lawn and sang and talked under the stars.

One night, Sean asked, "How can God be in control when it seems like He isn't?"

Jen had grown up in a Christian home; Sean had not. Jen and I had talked several times about her relationship with Sean and about his questions of faith—questions which were always thought provoking.

That night we talked about how God could be in control even when it appears He isn't. We also kicked around the purpose of life.

"I think," Sean stated, "that the purpose of life is to work hard, make money, provide for your family, and enjoy life."

"Where is God in that, Sean?" I challenged. "The purpose needs to be decided by the Designer not the designed. I believe the purpose of life is to know God and enjoy Him forever. God wants us to know Him—to have a relationship with Him. He wants us to reflect to others how great He is."

He didn't quite buy it, but I could tell his wheels were spinning. Sean promised to think about what I had said.

Jen told me that Sean spent most of the summer considering the claims of Christ.

The summer ended and Jen went to college in San Diego. Sean would drive down to see her most weekends. She would take him to her college church. Sean kind of liked the church, but he liked being anywhere with Jen.

One weekend, Sean had to work. He didn't make plans to go to San Diego. He got off early and decided to surprise Jen at her church. He got up at four A.M. on Sunday and drove for five hours. He got to the church on time, only to discover that Jen was not there. (She had gone to her friend's church.) Sean decided to not waste time looking for her and went into the church service. He had met the pastor and felt some connection with him. At the close of the sermon, the pastor asked if anyone needed to meet God personally.

Sean felt himself moving forward. With the pastor's help, he prayed to accept Christ as his Savior and Lord. Immediately, he felt a sense of peace. He had found forgiveness and purpose! He was filled with joy—so much that he felt like dancing!

After talking to the pastor for a few minutes, he ran to his car to go find Jen. His '65 Mustang had not been driven that fast since his racing days in high school. He was thrilled. *What will Jen think? Will she be surprised? Will she be mad because she wasn't there when it happened? I wonder.* Sean knew that she would celebrate with him.

It didn't take long for him to find her on campus.

As Sean walked across the campus lawn, Jen noticed that something was different about him. He walked differently. His head was held high, and he had a spring in his step that she had seldom seen, certainly not recently. *What was going on?*

"What are you doing here?" She ran and hugged him. She then pushed him back at arm's length, stared into his eyes, and demanded a response.

"I had to come—"

"But I thought you were working?"

"Got off early and went to your church."

"You what?!"

"Yeah, I went, by myself, and listened to the sermon and I BECAME A CHRISTIAN!"

"AAAHHH!" Jan shrieked. Tears quickly formed in her eyes. *I can't believe it! For years I pray for him, give him books, answer his questions, and invite him, and he does this without me. He does this on his own. How could he?* "That's great. I am so excited! About time," she kidded as she pulled him in close.

"I know. About time."

Jen recovered from the shock and introduced Sean to all her friends. She wanted them to meet the "new" Sean.

The two went out to dinner and talked about what Christ meant to each of them.

Finally, a conversation of spiritual substance! mused Jen.

They talked about how Sean's discovery could positively affect their relationship. Jen had been toying with the need to break up with him because he wasn't a believer. *But now, things were different. She could imagine a future with Sean. She could picture them being married.*

They talked about the possibility of life together as a married couple. Their love had never been stronger, nor had any one day seemed any longer.

Before they knew it, it was midnight and Sean had been up since four A.M. He walked Jen to her dorm, kissed her goodnight, and said, "I love you."

"I love you Sean, and now I can love you forever! Thanks for coming today, and thanks for making that decision today. And thanks for letting me celebrate it with you."

This is wonderful! Finally we have a common foundation in Christ.

Sean and Jen had spent the entire day talking about Christ and how they could grow in their love for Him and for each other.

Sean pulled the Mustang onto Interstate 5. "What a day!" He clapped his hand against the steering wheel. *Twenty-one hours ago I was driving here, hopeless and confused. I had no clue why I was here. Now, I know it is to enjoy God and help others know Him too.* "What a day!"

He headed north in his faithful Mustang. It was just a few miles outside San Diego that his car crashed into the center divider, instantly killing him. He had lived one day totally dedicated to give God glory, and God took him home!

> I want to know Christ and the power of his resurrection
> and the fellowship of sharing in his sufferings, becoming
> like him in his death (Phil. 3:10).

Sean discovered the purpose of life is to know Christ. Even though he died, he experiences life forever because of the power of Christ's Resurrection.

He is now like Him.

RESPONSE

1. What do you think about Sean's story?

2. What would you say to a friend who asked, "How can God be in control?"

3. How would you feel if you were Jen:
   ▶ when Sean surprises her with the news?
   ▶ when she hears about his death?

4. What does it mean to have a "common foundation in Christ?"

5. How do we *share in Christ's suffering?*

A LETTER TO MY SON

Dear Son,

Sean had so many fine qualities: he was an excellent student, a talented athlete, an engaging conversationalist, and a hard worker. He was mature beyond his years. Even with all of these assets, he was still searching.

He needed to meet Christ.

All the grades, the brassy MVP awards, the deep discussions, and success at work will not answer the questions plaguing every man: *Why am I here? What difference do I make?*

Sean spent a summer searching. And he found out.

Just in time.

Can you be sure you are ready? You have no guarantees that you will finish high school. That you will graduate from college. I am sure the last thing on Sean's mind was dying.

You never know.

Are you ready? If Jesus were to ask you today, "Why should I let you into My heaven?" what would you say to Him?

Let's talk about it. I want to make sure you are ready. And to make things perfectly fair, you can ask me the same question.

With eternity on my mind,

Dad

JOURNAL

Respond to the letter by writing your own thoughts in the section below. Parents may want to use Tim's letters as a model for their own.

_____

_____

_____

_____

_____

_____

_____

_____

_____

▶ CONNECTION ◀

Go to a wrecking yard and see if you can find a supersmashed car. Purchase something off of one of the wrecked cars: a gearshift knob; a tail-light; a mirror, etc.

Read Galatians 2:20 and discuss:

▶ What does it mean *to live for Christ? To die for Christ?*

▶ What would you say if Christ asked you, "Why should I let you into My heaven?"

▶ Can someone know, for sure, that they are "saved"? Read Ephesians 2:8-10.

Make a memorial from your wrecking yard treasure that helps you keep in mind to "live is for Christ and to die is gain." Consider integrating Galatians 2:20 or Ephesians 2:8-10 into your design.

CHAPTER 12

LOSERS

You really feel like a loser when:
▶ You wake up in the morning and find out your eyelids are stuck together with that stuff stronger than Super Glue.

▶ You check yourself out in the mirror, first thing in the morning, and blink as you think, *Do I really look that bad?* You blink again to discover you do.

▶ You have a rebellious nose hair that pokes out all day.

▶ You brush your teeth, gargle, floss and rinse, and your mouth still feels like four-week-old gym socks.

▶ A huge zit, the size of Mount Everest, erupts on your nose, and today is Picture Day.

▶ Your mom has washed your new baggy pants and they shrank in the dryer. Now they fit like leotards.

▶ You are starved and late for school and all there is to eat is FiberGram cereal—made from tree bark and shredded walnut shells.

▶ On the way out the door to school you realize you forgot to do the assignment for mean Mr. Butner, the teacher who gives you detention. You will have to sit near his desk while he eats his smelly liver sandwich.

▶ You trip going up the stairs in front of the Senior Quad causing the entire senior class to break out in uncontrollable laughter.

All of these add up to one BAD day! And it's only noon! So what should your attitude be when you feel like a loser?

Option 1: Take it out on everybody else.

Option 2: Blame somebody.

Option 3: Throw a pity party.

Option 4: Accept it and learn from it.

Which one would you select? It may not be the most popular, but

Option 4 is the right answer. Scripture tells us that we can actually learn from trials.

> Consider it pure joy, my brothers, whenever you face trials of many kinds, because you know that the testing of your faith develops perseverance. Perseverance must finish its work so that you may be mature and complete, not lacking anything (James 1:2-4).

We can each learn joy and perseverance when we are having a bad day. Joy isn't happiness. Happiness depends on "happenings" and comes from the same word. To be happy, certain positive things need to be happening.

Joy is different. *Joy is the continual confidence that God is in control of the details of my life.* Your life could be full of hassles and heartaches, and you can still have joy. In the midst of a trial you can have joy. Why? Because you know that your faith is being tested. Our faith is like a muscle; it needs to be worked out. Faith needs to be tested. When it is tested it gets stronger.

Have you met a person with a strong faith? Chances are, he or she has been through a lot of testing. You don't just have a strong faith because you want it. You need to develop it through testing (exercise).

Once we respond in joy when we face a trial (or a bad day), we learn not to give up but to hang in there. This is a quality we call *perseverance.* A person with perseverance is a person who works through the pain. Athletes who excel have perseverance. They have learned to work through the pain; they don't quit. In fact, some coaches say, "Embrace the pain," or "No pain, no gain."

Some days are painful and make you want to quit. Those are the days you need to look not at your circumstances, but at God. Remember that He is in control of the details of your life. He will help you deal with the hassles of the day. He can be your source of joy when everything seems such a pain. When you feel like a loser, remember Christ. He didn't wimp out and say, "The pain is too great. The cross is too uncomfortable." He stuck it out. His perseverance led to victory.

Sometimes the only difference between losers and winners is their willingness to hang in there.

RESPONSE

1. Complete the following: "I hate it when . . ."

2. Describe one of your bad days.

3. What does "Consider it pure joy when you face trials" look like? Describe how you would actually do this.

4. Joy is defined as *the continual confidence that God is in control of the details of my life.* Does this seem possible to you? What do you think of this definition?

5. How have you learned perseverance?

"It's one thing to try and fail, and another thing to fail to try."

A LETTER TO MY SON

Dear Son,

Today started out badly for you and only got worse! You had to give an oral report first period, and you are sure you did an awful job. You walked up to a group during break time, started to say something, and they looked at you as if you had just landed from Mars. Was it your skin? Had a zit popped up? Was it something you said? Why can't you ever feel confident and secure with what you are saying or doing or wearing? You still have to face P.E., and that ties your stomach in knots of worry. The thought of others seeing you trying to do pull-ups stresses you out. When you have to do tests in P.E., your body acts as though none of its parts are related!

We all have days like this—days when we are painfully aware of everything we do and say, days when we wonder what others are thinking about us. This is called *feeling self-conscious.* What we often fail to realize is that others aren't usually paying that much attention to us. They are far too busy worrying about how *they* look to *us!*

At times like these it seems the harder you try, the worse it gets. But actually you are not blowing it at all—you are just blowing it out of proportion.

Elijah, one of God's prophets, had a similar experience. Elijah was running away from an evil queen, Jezebel, who was trying to kill him. "I have had enough, Lord," he said. "I am the only one left (on God's side), and now they are trying to kill me too!" God told Elijah he was blowing this out of proportion.

He told him to get up and try again, and by the way there were still seven thousand faithful people in Israel. (You can read about this in I Kings 19.)

It's easy to blow things out of proportion when you have your eyes on yourself and your circumstances. That's what happened to Elijah. That is what happens to us.

Dear son, here are some ideas to help you get through days like these. First, understand that you may not be seeing yourself clearly. It's as if you are going through a house of mirrors at a carnival. You see yourself a dozen different ways, but they are all distorted. They don't reflect the real you. Once you are home, standing before your own mirror, you see a clear reflection. You have to get away from the distorted mirrors.

Second, remember that everyone else is just as concerned with himself or herself as you are. They probably aren't even noticing you because they are preoccupied with themselves.

Third, keep in mind God's picture of you. He has a portrait of you as a mature, godly young man. He will help you as you grow to match that picture.

> For the Lord will be your confidence and will keep your foot
> from being snared (Prov. 3:26).

Think of God, your Heavenly Father, with a picture of you in His wallet. He is proud of you. He loves you and accepts you. "Hey," He says to Saint Peter, "Have you seen my son? I am proud of him."

The Lord is our confidence.

Your fellow struggler,
Dad

JOURNAL

Respond to the letter by writing your own thoughts here. Parents may want to use Tim's letter as a model for their own.

_____

_____

_____

_____

_____

_____

_____

_____

_____

◆ CONNECTION ◀

Clean out your closets and drawers of clothes you don't wear anymore. See who can get the most clothes to give away: parent or teen. Take them to a thrift store (Salvation Army, Goodwill, or Rescue Mission). Donate the old clothes, and then spend thirty minutes and $5.00 each shopping for something you want. Afterward, talk about your new item, how you don't even need the clothes you gave away, and what would it be like to shop at a thrift store everyday. Would that be a _bad_ day or a _good_ day?

CHAPTER 13

WHEN YOU FEEL ALONE

Are you lonely? Do you ever feel alone in your role as a leader?"
I was shocked by the question. Ron was being very direct. I
had only known him for a few months, and now he was going
for the jugular. He was interrogating me about the forbidden topic. It's
okay to talk about sex, death, and taxes, but don't talk about loneliness!

I was caught off guard. *Should I pretend that I wasn't lonely and deny it
(as I had for years)? Besides, how could I be lonely? Thousands of people know
me!* I decided to risk authenticity. "Yeah. At times . . . sure. I guess you
could say that. Sometimes it's lonely being a leader. I mean, people surround me, but I'm always in my role as a pastor, leader, counselor, author,
and speaker. Sometimes I need to be 'just Tim.'"

"Would you like to be in a men's group with me?" Ron asked.

I studied him for a few seconds. I was impressed with his bravado, but
he was quite different from me. I wasn't sure I wanted to be in a group
with him. He was small, pale, and not very athletic. He spent his free time
indoors. *Why would I want to be in a group with him?*

"What kind of group were you thinking about?"

"A small group of about four guys. We could meet weekly for prayer
and maybe work through a book. Have you done this before?"

"Yes," I heard myself say.

"Was it a positive experience?"

Pleasant memories flooded my head. Toast, coffee, and eggs quickly
came to mind. I fondly thought of the guys I used to meet with at
Denny's for our small group and the Grand Slam Breakfast. "Oh yeah, I
used to do it all the time. I guess I got out of the habit. Yes, let's start a
group." I wasn't sure what I was getting into.

It was difficult for me to be real with Ron. It would have been easier to pretend that I wasn't lonely. *Why should I take the risk to be authentic?*

We began meeting weekly. Our group met to stimulate each other toward love and good deeds (Hebrews 10:24). I learned an important lesson: *Taking the risk to be real is better than the isolation of pretending.*

As guys, we are nervous about this topic. Most guys don't know how to grow a true friendship with another guy. Guys don't know how to be a friend. As a result, we are lonely.

When we hear the word *friend*, it scares us. It brings to mind obligations, commitments, vulnerability, and intimacy. We are also afraid of being too close; *I don't want anyone thinking I'm gay or anything.*

Guys can have close relationships without becoming homosexuals. True friendship doesn't have to be a burden. It doesn't have to be possessive or weird or sexual.

Another reason we pull away from friendships is because they require work. A worthwhile friendship requires investment. Most guys have acquaintances, but the commitment doesn't go beyond the surface level. They really don't know each other beyond work, school, or the playing field. Being a true friend means reaching out to another, connecting with him, establishing a friendship, and working to grow that relationship over time.

RESPONSE

1. How would you define *loneliness?*
2. Why is it risky to be real with others?
3. What are three or four qualities that you like in a friend?
4. Read Hebrews 10:24. How can this verse help in your friendships?
5. What are some ways we can invest in a friendship?

A LETTER TO MY SON

Dear Son,

The ironic thing about loneliness is that you can feel all alone and be surrounded by people. Loneliness does not mean being alone. Loneliness is the pain or sadness we feel when we are missing meaningful relationships.

We were designed for relationship. God is a relating God. He made us to relate to Him and to each other. God's design was for us to enjoy perfect (not just good) relationships. God said about Adam, "It is not good for the man to be alone" (Gen. 2:18).

We don't enjoy perfect relationships because of separation. What causes this separation? At least two things:

Circumstances cause separation. Rejection, a change in schedules, moving, divorce, and death cause us to be separated from those we care about.

Choices cause separation. Sometimes we are more concerned about what we need and ourselves. We make choices that help us, but they may hurt the relationship. We also make choices that protect us. We may prefer loneliness to disappointment. *I don't want to become friends because they may let me down.* We might choose to keep our relationships shallow so we don't get hurt. Some choices we make are excuses for avoiding real relationships. Some people choose to be too busy with sports, school, or work to have time to develop friendships.

I have many acquaintances and a few friends. What does it take to move from just knowing someone to becoming friends? I think it takes at least five essential elements for guys to develop an iron-sharpens-iron relationship with each other.

1. Having a desire to connect.

You must be willing to leave the cultural myth of the independent, macho stud in order to discover the value of a friendship with another guy. We can't do it alone; we really do need each other. Trying to be the Marlboro man riding along by himself is dangerous and lonely.

2. Being secure.

It is risky to try to develop a friendship; he might reject you. You will need to be willing to deal with the fears and risks of friendship and to be secure in what you believe. You will need to know when to stand your ground and when to walk away. There will be disagreements among friends, but differing points of view do not have to terminate a relationship. In fact, they often strengthen them.

3. Having fun together.

Guys need to laugh together if they are going to develop a friendship. Fun creates a shared experience. It could be sharing a joke or doing something you both enjoy. If guys are going to grow strong friendships, they will need to log in some fun times together. The reality is, guys won't put work into a friendship they don't enjoy.

4. Being real.

Sometimes we are afraid to be real, so we pose as if we have it all together. Posing this way keeps us from discovering our true selves. Being real helps us get to know the real person; it helps us be truthful. Most guys are dying for a friend who will let them be themselves and still accept them. When we are real, we are allowing truth to be at the core of our friendship.

5. Being comfortable with emotions.

We have emotions; we might as well get used to them. In fact, we should learn to get comfortable with our emotions and use them to understand ourselves and others. If two guys are going to work on a friendship, they will undoubtedly encounter some emotions. Emotions are normal responses to the environment around us, so talk about your emotions with your friends. It will help you grow closer and increase trust.

Son, I hope you are able to develop a friendship that shows these qualities. If you do, you will discover it is a valuable treasure. I also hope that we will be able to have a relationship that is meaningful and has these five qualities. I want to make the investment of time and effort. It may even cost some money, but you are worth it.

Still, I may not always be available to you. What can you do then? Seek Christ. He understands what it is like to be lonely. Read Matthew 26:36-45 to see how He handled a tough time when all of His friends deserted Him. A relationship with Christ can help your feelings of loneliness. You were designed to have a relationship with Him. Without it, you will always feel that something is missing. Christ fulfills the emptiness. He promises to be there when others bail out on you: "I will never leave you or forsake you."

I hope to follow Christ's example and always be there for you.

Love,
Dad

JOURNAL

Respond to the letter by writing your own thoughts in the section below. Parents may want to use Tim's letter as a model for their own.

_____

_____

_____

_____

_____

_____

_____

_____

_____

➡ CONNECTION ⬅

Write out Hebrews 10:24 on an index card. On the back of the card, describe the three or four qualities you want in a friend. Go out to breakfast. Choose a place where you will be comfortable and can discuss the Response questions. Make sure you take time to talk about what you wrote on the card. For instance, ask: "How can we spur each other on to love and good deeds?"

Suggestion: to allow more time consider a Saturday or Sunday breakfast.

CHAPTER 14

STAND AND DELIVER

Have you ever heard adults say to you, "These are the best years of your life, enjoy them"?

Doesn't it make you want to respond, "If these are the *best* years, why go on?"

And they wonder what contributes to teenage suicide.

Adults also say, "Teenagers today face so many challenges and pressures."

Well—which is it? A fun time or a hassle?

I think the truth is in the middle. Being a teenager means experiencing some real fun times, but it also means having some very real problems. I am not sure why adults spin a tale about how great the teen years are. Maybe they have selective memory about their own teen experience, forgetting some of the most difficult stuff.

The truth is, the teen years can be a time of insecurity, filled with worry about the way you look, with anxiety about school, sports, and activities, and with despair over your social life (or lack of one).

Somebody once compared the teenage years to being on a roller coaster. It might be fun at first, but if you get sick, all you want to do is get off. Meanwhile, everyone keeps telling you what a great ride it is!

Once we took the youth group to Magic Mountain Amusement Park. I noticed that the teens split into two basic groups: those who wanted to ride the roller coasters and those who didn't. I was surprised to see that Jeff wasn't with the "Coaster Crew." Typically, he was always ready for action. Jeff was a sixteen year old who had totaled a mountain bike, a motor scooter, and a Bronco all in one year! But he didn't want to go on the Viper.

"Why don't you want to go on the roller coaster?" I asked.

"Those kinds of rides make me sick," he said without embarrassment.

"Did you go on the Viper?"

"Nah, I was with my daughter and she didn't want to go." The truth was, I was afraid to go! I wimped out under pressure. Even adults experience peer pressure and cave in to it sometimes.

Later that day, Brooke said, "Dad, let's go on those rockets again, okay?"

"You go on ahead. I need to get something to drink." I wimped out again. I was afraid that I would get sick or twist my neck. But I made an excuse.

I think I should have learned a lesson from Jeff and just said, "I don't want to go." But I didn't.

When you think about it, the roller coaster imagery works for the teenage years. It captures the anticipation, the worry, the anxiety, the thrills, the highs, and the lows of a roller coaster.

Have you ever watched people get off a killer roller coaster? They are fun to watch. Some step out and walk away like they are climbing out of their car—no problem! Another person waits for two minutes, rubs his eyes, and tries to catch his breath. When he tries to stand up, the blood rushes to his head and he gets dizzy. He drops back to his seat. When he finally lumbers out of the roller coaster, he walks like a drunk and stumbles down the stairs.

By the way, who designs these places? Some sadistic architect? They always put stairs or steep walks leading down from these killer rides. The dizzy, nauseated riders can barely navigate the slope or the steps!

Anyway, there are two responses to a roller coaster ride: some people get out as though it's no problem, and others can barely walk.

The same is true for being a teenager. Sometimes you will look cool and walk as if you are totally in control, but at other times, you will feel like a complete idiot. The ups and downs of being a teenager can make you want to get off the ride soon. But I want to give you some good news: *You are not alone!*

As you encounter the highs and lows of your teen years, you may feel like, *nobody is feeling the way I do.* The fact is, lots of people feel exactly the way you do. That is why we need friends. Who wants to feel all alone?

As I see it, there are three types of influences:

1. positive influences

2. negative influences

3. neutral influences

When adults talk about "teen problems" and "peer pressure," they are usually thinking about *negative influences*. "Stop hanging around that Fonzerrilli guy. He's a bad influence. He rides a motorcycle and wears a leather jacket. He's trouble."

You get the picture. But what about "positive peer influence"?

CHRISTA'S HOBBY

Christa loved to make jewelry. She became quite good at it. One day she asked Shawna, "Would you like to get together and learn how? I will show you."

Shawna had been admiring Christa's new earrings. "Sure, that would be fun."

Christa wanted to have a positive influence on Shawna, a new girl at our youth group. Shawna had been spending many of her afternoons drinking beer with some guys and becoming sexually involved. Christa wanted to get her out of this risky behavior and offer a healthier alternative.

Shawna jumped at the chance. She really got into making jewelry, and in a few short weeks she and Christa had made lots of it and were able to sell some and make quite a profit.

As they made jewelry, Christa would ask questions, talk about her relationship with God, and share Scripture that had helped her. She was discipling Shawna as they made jewelry! Christa was a positive peer influence on Shawna.

Positive peer pressure means:

▶ Encouraging a friend to go out for a sport when he is afraid

▶ Organizing a study group to prepare for a test

▶ Helping someone finish some chores at home so he can go out

▶ Inviting someone (who usually is overlooked) to join your group when you do something

▶ Rallying your friends together to help someone in need

When you think about it, positive peer pressure can be just as strong as negative peer pressure.

Being a teenager doesn't mean you have to have a difficult time. It doesn't mean that you will have any more problems than any other stage of life. So why do people say being a teen is so tough? Maybe the teen years aren't any different from other stages of life, but it just *feels* that way. My theory is that the teen years are like other times in life but with the volume cranked up! Everything seems louder and more dramatic. The highs are higher and the lows seem lower.

I think the teen years have received some bad press from adults because some adults have focused on negative peer pressure and a few "bad apples" in the bushel. But what about positive peer influence and the overwhelming majority of teens who are "good apples"?

TAKING A STAND

We have talked about two kinds of influences in our lives, but what is a *neutral* influence? *A neutral influence is something that shapes you but not in a moral sense.* Let's say your friend loves Pecan Praline ice cream. Every time you go to his house, he serves you some. You may grow to like Pecan Praline ice cream. Is this negative peer pressure?

No.

Is it positive peer pressure?

No.

It's neutral.

To help you deal with the pressure you will face, consider three critical questions:

What do I stand for?

What do I stand against?

Who will stand with me?

A Scripture passage that might help you as you consider these questions is in Matthew:

You are a light of the world. A city on a hill cannot be hidden. Neither do people light a lamp and put it under a bowl. Instead they put it on its stand, and it gives light to everyone in the house. In the same way, let your light shine before men, that they may see your good deeds and praise your Father in heaven (Matt.5:14-16).

As believers, we are to stand for the light.

We are to stand against the darkness.

We are to stand together as believers, as a witness to the watching world. By taking a stand for the light, you could help some of your friends who could be lost in darkness. Take a stand for what you believe. It could make a difference in somebody else's life.

RESPONSE

1. What do you think about the myth that the teen years are the best years of your life?

2. Do you think the teen years are like a roller coaster? Why or why not?

3. Have you ever noticed positive peer influence like Christa had on Shawna? Describe it.

4. What are some things that you stand for? Stand against?

5. Whom can you count on to stand with you? Why?

A LETTER TO MY SON

Dear Son,

Somebody once told me, "If you don't stand for something, you will fall for anything." I think it is good advice. We need a cause to rally around. We need a mission to help give us a sense of purpose. But I have also observed that we need something more. It's not enough to stand *for* something; we also need to *stand against* some things.

To put it in sports language, you need a defense as well as an offense.

There are all kinds of influences out there that are trying to shape you into their mold. They want to change you. They want to make you into something that you are not. It is not enough to wink at them and say, "I stand for this." That approach is too naive.

In order to stand up for something, you will need to stand against anything that challenges it. You will need to face the enemy.

> Don't copy the behavior and customs of this world, but let
> God transform you into a new person by changing the way
> you think. Then you will know what God wants you to do,

and you will know how good and pleasing and perfect his
will really is (Rom. 12:2, NLT).

Certain behaviors and customs of the world are hostile to the things of God.
They aren't neutral or positive. They are negative; they are the enemy. These are
the things we need to stand against. For instance, Shawna was getting drunk and
was sexually involved with guys. This is behavior from the world, not from God.
Christa helped her by getting her mind on other things, on godly things. God
changes us into new people by changing the way we think.

Renew your mind. Stand and deliver!

JOURNAL

Respond to the letter by writing your own thoughts in the section
below. Parents may want to use Tim's letter as a model for their own.

_____

_____

_____

_____

_____

_____

_____

_____

_____

➡ CONNECTION ⬅

Go on a night hike up a hill or mountain. Bring your flashlight and
Matthew 5:14-16 written on an index card. Read the verses and discuss
what you observe from this position. How does this perspective relate to
being courageous enough to "stand and deliver"?

CHAPTER 15

CAN I TAKE MY BRAIN TO THE CAR WASH?

I received one of those cool hand-held computers for Christmas. I spent part of Christmas day entering data from my trusty, old-fashioned, leather-bound Daytimer. A few days later, I was having lunch with a friend. I wanted to show off my new "toy."

"Here, look, I even have your name, phone, address, and e-mail address in it, Bob."

"That's great," he said, looking at the entry. "I am impressed. Looks real high tech," he added sarcastically.

I glanced at the entry. I had misspelled his name. It read *Boob!*

So much for leading-edge technology, if the data input person messes up!

It reminded me of an old computer-related slogan: garbage in, garbage out. That means what you get out of your computer is largely determined by what you put into it.

The same is true of your mind. What you put into your mind will have an impact on what comes out. If you allow garbage to enter your mind, expect that it will come out through your words or behavior. Our minds are more like a computer than a recycler.

I have talked to some guys who have the recycler mentality.

"It doesn't matter what comes into my mind, I just filter out what I don't want and keep the rest."

"So the bad stuff doesn't harm you?"

"Nah, I just recycle it into good stuff."

I wish that the recycle approach worked, but everything we know about how our minds work proves otherwise. We are affected by all information coming into our brains.

The Bible tells us that your mind matters. What input you allow will influence nearly everything that happens in your life. Proverbs 23:7 reminds us, "As he thinks within himself, so he is" (NASB).

We become what we think about. If we think about positive and healthy things, we will become positive and healthy. If we choose to think about negative and unhealthy things, we will become negative and unhealthy. You are what you think.

Let's consider some of the sources for mental input. These can be positive or negative.

TELEVISION

Not all TV is harmful, but it isn't all neutral either. Popular teen shows feature teens that have sex, drink beer, defy authority, engage in witchcraft, and think their parents are losers. The average teenager watches over thirteen hundred hours of TV a year. He will see over ten thousand commercials a year.

Sometimes the commercials are more persuasive than the program. After a few hours of watching, you feel like you are missing out. You may actually feel dissatisfied. This is the goal of advertisers—to make you feel like you are incomplete or out-of-it without their product. For instance:

▶ You need Air Jordans to play basketball like Michael Jordan.

▶ You need Tostitos to have attractive babes come on to you in the Laundromat.

▶ You need Michelob to have smiling friends and a night that is something special.

▶ You need Trojan prophylactics if you are going to "be a man."

▶ You need Gap khakis to have a herd of dancing, gender-blender friends.

Without these critical, must-have products you are a loser (according to the advertisers).

What about MTV?

Music videos, whether they are MTV, VH1, or country, can be all over the map. Some are fun and innocent, and others are demonic and vile. My suggestion? Keep the remote close and be prepared to use it. *Which videos are okay?* The ones you would watch if Jesus Christ were sitting next to you. I'm serious—because if you are a Christian, He is sitting next to you!

PORNOGRAPHY

Thanks to the Internet, porn has never been more available. It used to be that guys would hide their *Playboy* magazines under their mattresses. Now, they have access to live chats with strippers, a wide range of photos, and a huge menu of perversions available on their computer screen.

Nobody will ever know! There's no evidence under the mattress. The temptation is powerful.

You might ask, "What's wrong with porn?" Here is what I would say:

1. It promotes a lustful fantasy life.
2. It dehumanizes women, making them into sexual objects.
3. It depersonalizes sex, depicting it as an act, not part of a loving relationship.
4. It can lead to perversion (like homosexuality) and to sexual addiction.
5. It causes you to withdraw from real relationships into fantasy.
6. It can lead to sexual violence. Most sex offenders are addicted to porn.
7. It goes against God's plan for us. (See Matthew 5:27-30.)

MUSIC

You might like rap, R&B, country, metal, hip hop, alternative, classic rock, punk, or some other form of music. Listening to some of the lyrics, I'd say that some of today's popular music is pornographic when it talks about sex, perversion, and "getting it." Some Christians say you shouldn't listen to any secular music. Others say, "anything goes."

How about listening selectively? Most of the seven things that make pornography wrong can also be said of some music. As you listen to *your* music, ask yourself:

▶ Do I believe what they are singing?
▶ Does it make God look good?
▶ Would I do it with Jesus here?
▶ Is it a wise use of my time?

Each of us has the ability to resist temptation, but sometimes we overload this ability and it does not work. It's not wrong to be tempted. We are all tempted. The problem comes when we give in to temptation.

If you think about it, you can probably identify something in your life that shows you are losing the battle with temptation. Let's think about some tips to resist temptation.

FIVE TIPS TO RESIST TEMPTATION

Tip 1: Be in the right place. There are certain places where it is too easy to give in to temptation. If you are in the right place, it will give you strength and knowledge to know and avoid the wrong places. For example, if you go to youth group Bible study, you may learn something that may help you avoid temptation.

Tip 2: Be with the right people. In junior high, I couldn't figure out why I had a chair in the principal's office with my name on it. You see, two of my friends were always getting into trouble. I was with them, so I got in trouble too. One day, as I sat in Mr. Baldwin's office, it hit me: *If I just don't hang around with these guys, I won't get in trouble!* Brilliant, huh?

Tip 3: Be ready to run when it gets hot. It was Joseph, a guy in the Old Testament, who taught me this technique to avoid the snare of temptation. You may remember the story: Joseph was working for Potiphar and really doing a great job. He received all kinds of promotions and honors. Potiphar really liked him. (This story is found in Genesis 39.)

One day, Mrs. Potiphar noticed that Joseph was a hunk. She tried to seduce him, but he saw what was happening, so he literally ran away from her, leaving his coat in her hot little hands.

Joseph had learned that there are times when temptation is so strong that we should not hang around to discuss it or think about it. Sometimes it's best to run now and think later.

Tip 4: Be alert and ready for sneak attacks. Temptation can be sneaky. You need to have your guard up and be alert. You can never tell from what angle temptation will come.

> Be self-controlled and alert. Your enemy the devil prowls around like a roaring lion looking for someone to devour. Resist him, standing firm in the faith (1 Peter 5:8-9).

The Devil is devious and wants to destroy your life. But he doesn't send you an e-mail that reads, "I am planning to attack you tomorrow night at the movies." The Devil wants to surprise you with a sneak attack. He won't give you a warning.

We stay alert by expecting the Devil to attack us in our weak spots. For example, I know I am weakest when I am tired, hungry, or hurt, so those are times that I need to be especially alert to temptation.

If we can stay alert, we can be prepared to resist temptation—the kind that comes from inside us and the kind that comes outside us.

Tip 5: Be in the Bible, and get it in you. Memorize Scripture and use it to defeat temptation. The Bible can be like a pocketknife that you can pull out and use to cut yourself free from the vines which entangle you and pull you into temptation.

> No temptation has seized you except what is common to man. And God is faithful; he will not let you be tempted beyond what you can bear. But when you are tempted, he will also provide a way out so that you can stand up under it (1 Cor. 10:13).

I was thirteen years old when I encountered this verse. I was at Eagle Lake camp, lying on my bunk in my teepee. Free time was ahead of me, but before I could go out on the lake in a canoe, my counselor made me memorize this verse. For some reason, I had difficulty with this verse. Every other day I quickly memorized and recited the verse of the day and went out to play, but not this verse. This verse was giving me trouble. It took me hours, but I finally got it. By the time I got to the canoes, I could only go for a few minutes. Free time was up and it started to rain.

I hate 1 Corinthians 10:13!

It put me in a bad mood the rest of the day. The next morning I woke up and realized what a helpful verse this could be for a teenager. I was glad I had memorized it. I was even glad my counselor made me learn it. (Well, maybe I wasn't so glad that week, but I was about two years later!) It has proven to be a lifesaver for me as a teenager and now as an adult.

RESPONSE

1. What do you think about what Tim says about TV, MTV, pornography, and music?

2. Discuss the Five Tips to Resist Temptation.

3. Which one of the Five Tips is the hardest for you? Why? Which one would be the most helpful for you?

4. How does memorizing Scripture help avoid temptation?

5. First Corinthians 10:13 talks about God providing a way out of temptation. What are some ways God provides these escape routes?

A LETTER TO MY SON

Dear Son,

The world tells us that we don't need rules and absolutes to be free. "Everybody do their own thing!" But can you imagine if everybody did that driving the freeways of L.A.? It would be a disaster! That's why we have rules. If the rules are appropriate, they actually lead to freedom. Psalm 119:32 tells us, "I run in the path of your commands, for you have set my heart free."

I like this verse because it teaches us that true freedom comes from obeying God's commands. When we "run in the path" of God's commands, we stay free from the temptations that try to control us. Our heart can be free from guilt because we did not give in to temptation. We can be free!

Temptation doesn't always have to win. God has promised to help us right in the middle of the temptation. One way God helps us is by giving us strength from His Word. Try memorizing 1 Corinthians 10:13 as your escape route from temptation. It reminds us that God won't let any temptation come into our lives that we can't handle. Now that's a promise that will be useful in your teenage years!

With you in the battle,
Dad

"I have kept my feet from every evil path so that I might obey your word" (Ps. 119:101).

JOURNAL

Respond to the letter by writing your own thoughts here. Parents may want to use Tim's letter as a model for their own.

_____

_____

_____

_____

_____

_____

_____

_____

_____

➡ CONNECTION ⬅

Go out to eat together (teen and parent). Enjoy conversation together and talk about some of the topics from this book. After dinner, ask to see the dessert tray, spend a minute talking and looking, but then don't order any! Talk about resisting temptation!

CHAPTER 16

MOUTH POWER

He is such a wimp! I can't believe he doesn't go pound that guy. What a woosie."

"Hey, here he comes. Let's give it to him."

"Hey, pansy! I heard Kyle is giving you a hard time. Why don't you take him on? Chicken?"

"Kyle is so lame. But you're a wimp if you don't punch his lights out for him dissin' you."

"Oh, he's just gonna walk on by. Are you in a hurry to get to ballet? Fag."

This was an actual high school conversation cleaned up for family use. The language on high school and middle school campuses can be brutal. It is usually vulgar. I don't have to tell you teens this, because you live with it. But the adults might be surprised to discover how coarsely some teens talk these days.

It seems that we have lost common sense in our culture when it comes to appropriate language. Words that used to be restricted to college locker rooms and R-rated movies are now flung around by fifth graders. What used to bring gasps and reactions now brings yawns as people look the other way. Swearing and bad language are so commonplace that we hardly notice.

Our culture has changed.

But God's Word hasn't.

"You shall not misuse the name of the LORD your God, for the LORD will not hold anyone guiltless who misuses His name" (Ex. 20:7). Most of us know the commandment, but have you ever asked yourself, *why is it that people use* Jesus Christ *or* God *as swear words?*

Because they are powerful words. *Swearing is the attempt of a weak person to speak with authority.* In some ways it does make sense to use

God's name instead of a person's. Can you imagine using the name *Billy* as a swearword? It wouldn't carry much weight! People must know that God's name is powerful, or they wouldn't use it when they swear.

Let's say your name is Billy. How would you like it if people, when they got mad, would spit out, "Billlee!" At first you might keep saying, "Yes, what do you want?" But after a while it would get old, and it would make you mad. You would probably respond with, "Don't use my name unless you want me!" The same is true with God and Jesus. We are not supposed to misuse their names.

> But I tell you, Do not swear at all: either by heaven, for it is
> God's throne; or by the earth, for it is his footstool. . . . Simply
> let your 'Yes' be 'Yes' and your 'No,' 'No' (Matt. 5:34-37).

If you catch yourself using God's name in swearing, you might want to ask yourself some questions:

1. Where did I learn to do this?
2. Am I copying someone I want to be like or trying to impress others?
3. Am I trying to sound cool or tough by swearing?
4. Since I am a Christian and have a relationship with God, how does misusing His name affect that relationship?

What about those other swearwords? You know, the ones that are called four-letter words and that are profane and obscene. Is it right for a Christian to let a few of these rip from time to time?

Think about your favorite bad word—the one that sometimes sneaks out of your lips. Got it in mind? (I have one that challenges me.) Let's see how our favorite bad words stack up against Scripture:

> Do not let any unwholesome talk come out of your
> mouths, but only what is helpful for building others up
> according to their needs, that it may benefit those who lis-
> ten (Eph. 4:29).

Use this Scripture passage as a checklist.
▶ Is it wholesome and pure?
▶ Does it help build others up and encourage them?
▶ Do people benefit by hearing me use that word?

▶ Do my words meet the needs of others?

The talk that comes out of our mouths reveals what is on our minds. If we are struggling with bad language it might be due to what is coming into our brains. If we are exposed to input from movies, music videos, and people, it will show up in how we talk—good or bad.

One of the best ways to influence your speech is to control what comes into your brain.

I recommend a good dose of Scripture every day to renew your mind and keep it fresh and clean. "Do not be conformed to this world, but be transformed by the constant renewal of your mind" (Rom. 12:1-2, RSV).

The world taints our brains with information that opposes what God wants. We need to rinse it away and be renewed with the positive truth of God's Word. If we do this, it will be reflected in our speech.

RESPONSE

1. Why do you think our culture is so casual about bad language?

2. What can we do when we hear someone use God's name in vain?

3. What would you say to a friend who constantly swears and uses God's name as a swearword?

4. Re-read all of the verses listed in this chapter. If you memorized these, what affect do you think it might have on your speech?

5. How can you use your speech to build others up?

A LETTER TO MY SON

Dear Son,

Whoever made up the saying "Sticks and stones may break my bones, but names will never hurt me" obviously never went to school! Names can become labels. They can follow you around from grade school, through middle school, and haunt you in the halls of high school. Some people never outlive their nicknames or labels that others give them.

What we say to others and what we call them can be very powerful. Can you think of a time when someone labeled you? Sometimes it's okay, but most of the time you don't want to get stuck with it. We need to be careful not to swear, use God's name uselessly, or hurt others with our words. How can we do that?

Don't simply view harmful speech as a pest, like ants at a picnic. Instead, consider hurtful speech as the enemy. Do all you can to oppose it and get rid of it. Don't just put up with it—eliminate it!

Here are some ways you can become The Eliminator when it comes to bad language:

1. Identify the enemy. Write the words you want to stop using on an index card.

2. Ask God to make you sensitive to these words and be aware of when you use them. Also ask Him to help you to erase them from your mind and lips.

3. Carry the card with you and record the number of times you say each word in one day. Make yourself put a check by each word every time you catch yourself saying it.

4. On the back of the card write a Scripture passage that you are trying to memorize. Start with Philippians 4:8. Concentrate on this verse throughout the day.

5. When you catch yourself swearing, stop and tell God you are sorry, thank Him for forgiving you, and then ask Him to help you stop. Review your memory verse. This is a garbage in—garbage out discipline. Instead of filling your mind with negative language, you are trying to renew your mind with God's Word.

6. Cross out a swearword on your card when you can get through a week without saying it.

7. Ask a friend to wink at you or tug on his left earlobe when he catches you swearing. (This beats him saying, "I thought you were going to stop swearing!")

8. Stop allowing the input of swearwords as much as you can. Watch your choice of movies, music, jokes, and even friends.

I will be there to help you too. If I hear you using bad language, I will point it out. And to be totally fair, if I blow it with swearing, let me know, preferably in private! Sometimes we don't even realize what we are saying. But words are too powerful and precious to be wasted.

Here's to helpful words,
Dad

JOURNAL

Respond to the letter by writing your own thoughts here. Parents may want to use Tim's letter as a model for their own.

_____

_____

_____

_____

_____

_____

_____

_____

_____

➧ CONNECTION ◀

Watch a rerun of an old TV show together (parent and teen), something like *I Love Lucy* or *I Dream of Jeannie.* Or rent a video of a positive, wholesome movie from an earlier time. Then watch a contemporary sitcom. Record in writing how many times the new show uses bad language or refers to something that goes against biblical standards.

Pop some popcorn and discuss the contrasts between the shows. Also discuss what you think you should do about watching the more recent sitcoms and shows.

CHAPTER 17

PRESSURE RELIEF

When I was ten, I used to lie on the grass in my backyard and gaze up at the clouds in the sky. I would make animals out of the shapes: lions, elephants, and sometimes a giraffe. I did this often. It was fun, and I didn't have anything else to do. We didn't have a TV. Video games weren't invented yet. I didn't have a stereo, VCR, CD player, or computer. For entertainment, I would stare at the clouds!

I was sharing this story with a group of middle school students, and one guy asked, "Cloud Gazer—is that out on Sega Genesis now?"

We live in a culture with lots of options. Life isn't as simple as it used to be. Thanks to technology we have all kinds of new sources of information. It takes more time to deal with these options, to make these choices. To get it all in we find ourselves speeding up. One of the characteristics of our culture is the rush we all seem to be in. Who has time to look at clouds?

I am sure you have noticed how hurried most adults are. They look busy and stressed. You probably can't figure out why they are always in such a rush.

Do you ever feel rushed? How do you feel when you are rushed?

Most parents I know feel that they don't have enough time to spend with their kids. They are looking for ways to slow down and connect with those they care about, especially their children. But we live in a culture addicted to the rush. We have a love affair with haste.

Cloud gazing isn't an Olympic sport. You simply kick back, pick a cloud, and imagine it to be whatever you want. No pressure! No competition! Maybe that's why cloud gazing is a fading pastime: it's not competitive enough. Not only can we get swept away in the rush of the culture, but we can also choke on all the competitiveness.

BRYCE

Bryce was a star swimmer. At fifteen he was setting age-group records. To keep his competitive edge, he would work out twice a day, at five A.M. and after school. I asked him why he did it.

"I feel the pressure to be the best and the only way I can be the best is to work harder than the rest."

Bryce swam two hours before school and three hours after, plus he did an hour of weights and cycling. After a few years of this intense schedule, it was no longer fun. He was very fast and was attracting a lot of attention and awards. If you watched him swim on Saturday, you would say, "Amazing! What a swimmer!"

I saw Bryce on Sundays; he was worn out and looked depressed.

Our society puts a big price tag on accomplishment. Being the best becomes the focus. Teens hear adults say, "Bigger is better," "Wealth provides choices," and "Power equals control." To get ahead, we feel we need to be competitive. After all, *it's survival of the fittest.* Play is out and competition is in.

Many of the teens I talk to complain about the competitive spirit they see in their parents. "They always have to be the best or have the best, or they aren't happy. It puts a lot of pressure on me too. They think I want the same thing, but I don't. I'm not that obsessed about it. I am more into having a good time with my close friends."

We are a culture obsessed with ourselves. Adults often talk to me about how self-focused teenagers are, but I see dozens of adults who are just as caught up in themselves.

As most things in life, this isn't all bad. We need to take care of ourselves, but we can overdo it. We can insulate ourselves from what is really important.

A few years ago a train derailed on the Pacific Coast in a nearby city. The neighborhood on the beach was evacuated and the Pacific Coast Highway was closed. The toxic chemicals spilled created a serious threat to the environment and human life.

I was talking to a teenager about it. "The toxic spill was pretty potent. It will keep people from their homes and work. The homeless in the riverbed had to leave too."

"It makes me really mad," he replied. "I can't go surf Rincon because of that stupid spill."

He could care less about the people and the environment. He only focused on how the disaster affected him, how it interrupted his surfing.

We tend to look at things in light of their effect on us. Sometimes, we approach our relationships with the motive, *What's in it for me?* It's hard not to think this way, because our culture encourages us to do so. How many music videos talk about doing something helpful for someone else? Most of them sing about grabbing lustfully all you can get.

The media darlings and the pop idols offer alternatives, but no models. They really don't provide us with helpful ways to deal with pressure.

HEAT CONTROL

You might be taking some heat to be like somebody else, to do what's cool or what your buddies are doing. They want you to *go with the flow.*

This is another source of pressure—*peer pressure.* When it comes to taking some heat, which are you: a thermometer or a thermostat?

A thermometer doesn't control anything; it just reports heat. It responds to the heat around it and reflects how hot it is.

A thermostat actually regulates the environment. It controls the heat around it.

Every person can become a thermostat. You can regulate the temperature of your environment: your school, your friends, your home, and your team.

But you can't do it alone. You need help.

> Don't copy the behavior and customs of this world, but be
> a new and different person with a freshness in all you do
> and think. Then you will learn from your own experience
> how His ways will really satisfy you (Rom. 12:2, TLB).

To escape the squeeze of this world, we need God's help. We need to offer our minds, bodies, and souls to Him. With Him in control of our lives we have the supernatural strength we need to regulate our environment instead of being controlled by it. With God's leadership and power we can become thermostats instead of thermometers. Our hope needs to be in Him, not the reaction and applause of our friends. God is the only one we can have confidence in. He is the only source of true and lasting satisfaction.

A relationship with God can help us endure the hurried race of our times. God is eternal. He is not in a hurry. He can help us get perspective on time. God can help us fight off the temptation to always be competitive. He loves us even when we lose. When we encounter the hassles of the day, God is there offering peace. When we are caught by the lust for material things, God offers contentment. And in a world that is uncertain and confused, we hear the Good Shepherd say, "I am the way, the truth, and the life. Follow me."

Response

1. Did you gaze at clouds as a child? What did you do when you had plenty of free time?

2. Why do people seem so rushed these days?

3. Why do you think there is so much emphasis on accomplishment and winning?

4. What are some ways you experience peer pressure?

5. Describe one practical way you can be a thermostat.

A Letter To My Son

Dear Son,

Let me level with you—peer pressure isn't just for teenagers. We experience it too as *old folks.* You don't hear too much about *forty-something peer pressure,* but it exists. We usually call it something else: "Keeping up with the Joneses," "Staying trendy," "Dressing in style," or "Providing for my family."

This may be discouraging to you, but peer pressure is not something you grow out of when you get older.

That is why it is good to learn how to deal with it now. You will develop some skills to deal with pressure, particularly peer pressure, and it will pay off throughout your life. The key is to discover self-confidence based on God's love for you. You can face challenging peer pressure and have victory. Negative peer influence is an enemy you can beat.

Don't underestimate your friends' influence. They are either helping you up or bringing you down. Imagine that you are in a boat and you fall out. A helpful friend extends his hand and pulls you back to safety. He helps you up. A hurtful friend is under the surface of the water and tries to pull you down. He would rather have your company to drown with him than to help you.

Ask yourself this question frequently: *Is my friend trying to help me up or bring me down?*

Sometimes it changes. Sometimes a friend who used to help you winds up changing and bringing you down. Be careful, because this can sneak up on you. Your trusted friend may go through a season when, instead of being a "bring you up" friend, he becomes a "drag you down" friend. What should you do then?

Be a *thermostat* not a *thermometer.*

Hang in there,
Dad

JOURNAL

Respond to the letter by writing your own thoughts in the section below. Parents may want to use Tim's letter as a model for their own.

_____

_____

_____

_____

_____

_____

_____

_____

➡ CONNECTION ⬅

Play-Doh Pressure

Get some Play-Doh or modeling clay for parent and teen. Begin by creating something that indicates some kind of pressure you are facing. Describe the pressure and your clay creation to each other. Then read Romans 12:1-2. One of the translations talks about the world "squeezing you into its mold." Discuss how you are like clay being pressured into something other than your true self. Then model a new creation that reflects being renewed in Christ and set free from the world's pressures. Fire the clay, or let it dry, and keep it in a place that will remind you to be a "new creation."

CHAPTER 18

PROVE IT, IF YOU LOVE HER

Why is God against sex? Why did He make me with all these urges and then tell me 'no'? I want to be holy, but I'm horny," confessed fourteen-year-old Kirk.

"God isn't against sex. He's excited about it. After all, He invented it! His concern is that we use sex as it was created to be used."

Kirk looked confused about my response. "What do you mean?"

"When we follow the Creator's instructions, we get the maximum enjoyment and fulfillment out of sex. When we ignore God's instructions and plans, we wind up feeling empty inside, and we miss the real joy of sex."

He looked sad. "My girlfriend and I messed up."

"Yeah, what happened?"

"We had sex. It really wasn't that much fun. It was kind of a let down. I felt dirty and guilty afterward. It wasn't like they show in the movies."

I thought about Kirk and the innocence he and his girlfriend had lost.

"I'm sorry to hear that."

"It really wasn't worth it."

"It usually isn't when we do things our way instead of God's way."

"So . . . what do I do now?"

I could see the confusion in his eyes. "Come to God, ask His forgiveness, and commit to do things His way."

"What is His way?"

"Kirk, God intended sex to be fun—and yes, thrilling! But He created us to best express love and enjoy sex within the security of marriage. Sex is more than 'making love,' it is an expression of love and self-control. When a husband and wife control themselves in such a way that they save sex for each other and no one else, then it becomes a very special, unique gift that they give each other."

"It's not so special if you are giving it away to everyone."

"Yeah, that's it. Sex in marriage develops a wonderful bond that is different from any other relationship. When sex is outside of marriage, this special bond is impossible. Outside of marriage, sex can become more of a noose than a bond."

"I know what you mean. I feel trapped in a relationship with my girlfriend because we did it."

"What's changed?"

"I don't like her as much. I don't respect her anymore. I don't respect myself. We fight all the time."

"I know what you mean. It reminds me of Tom, another fourteen year old. He told me, 'We started foolin' around a little, and before you knew it, we were going all the way. It was kind of exciting at first, but it made us both feel guilty and trapped. It was almost like being hooked on a drug—every time we got together we started messin' around. After a while it really wasn't that much fun, but we couldn't stop.'"

Kirk's eyes began to moisten. "I know how he feels. The pull is so strong, it's hard to resist. What did you tell Tom?"

"I told him that he was experiencing guilt and pain because he was trying to live according to Tom's way, not God's. I showed him what God says:

> It is God's will that you should be sanctified: that you should avoid sexual immorality; that each of you should learn to control his own body in a way that is holy and honorable (1 Thes. 4:3-4).

"I asked Tom if he wanted to be holy and close to God. He told me he did. I told him he couldn't have it both ways; he would have to give up his idol of sex to honor God."

"Sex can be an idol?"

"If it takes our focus off God and it captures our emotions, it is an idol."

"I never thought of it that way."

"But see how much worry, attention, and stress you have over being sexually active?"

"Absolutely. I am obsessed over it."

"Then it has become an idol."

"What can I do?"

"God wants us to *avoid* sexual immorality. It's not enough just to keep from doing it; we should be active in avoiding situations that may lead to sexual sin. This includes all sorts of things, such as watching movies, visiting Internet sites, or reading books and magazines that cause you to think about sex. Sometimes we need to actually run away from situations that may tempt us sexually. Remember how Joseph had to run away from the clutches of Potiphar's wife?"

"Oh yeah, I remember that story. I guess the Bible does know what we are dealing with."

"It's very relevant. In fact, here is another Scripture passage you can use to resist sexual temptation: 'Flee the evil desires of youth, and pursue righteousness, faith, love and peace, along with those who call on the Lord out of a pure heart' (2 Tim. 2:22).

"Controlling your body is *your* responsibility. No one else can do it for you. God holds you responsible for what you do with your sex life. To be involved sexually before marriage is against His will. But God never asks us to do anything that He doesn't give us the strength to do."

RESPONSE

1. What do you think it means to "lose your innocence" by being sexually active?

2. Why do you think God made sex fun? Why does He restrict it to marriage?

3. Why do you think both Kirk and Tom felt trapped?

4. Do you agree that sex can become an idol?

5. What are some practical ways we can *flee* sexual temptation?

A LETTER TO MY SON

Dear Son,

I hope these stories about Kirk and Tom will be helpful to you. As you can tell, sex is an important part of your life. It is a powerful, God-given part of who we are. Decisions that you make in this area of your life can have a huge impact on your whole life. They can influence your life now and in the future. That's why it is important to me to talk with you about these issues.

> No temptation has seized you except what is common to man. And God is faithful; he will not let you be tempted beyond what you can bear. But when you are tempted, he will also provide a way out so that you can stand up under it (1 Cor. 10:13).

God asks us to not be involved sexually prior to marriage. In this verse, He promises to provide an escape route to even the most attractive temptations. Some people say, "I had to give in to the temptation. It was just too powerful!" According to this verse, as Christians we don't have to allow temptation to suck us into its power. God won't allow us to be tempted beyond what we are able to resist. It is a promise—a promise from God.

Knowing that God will help us with every kind of temptation makes it a little easier to stand up to our friends who might be saying, "Go for it! Everybody does it! Go all the way, nobody will know. Come on, you don't want to be the only virgin in school, do you?"

Knowing that God "will not let you be tempted beyond what you can bear" can also help you when you are getting desperate to have a girlfriend or have sex. You don't have to give into the temptation to use seductive strategies or manipulation to win her. God may show you another way or another girl. Somebody once said, "You keep a relationship going with what got it started." In other words, if you first got the relationship going with sex, then your girlfriend is going to expect a sex-oriented relationship. But if you first attract a girl with your sense of humor and your love for Christ, you will enjoy a relationship centered on laughter and a common Lord.

Just a personal note to end with: struggling with sexual issues doesn't end in your teen years; it only begins there! But the lessons you learn as a teen can help you the rest of your life.

A fellow learner,
Dad

JOURNAL

Respond to the letter by writing your own thoughts here. Parents may want to use Tim's letter as a model for their own.

_____

_____

_____

_____

_____

_____

_____

_____

_____

➡ CONNECTION ◀

Sex, Lies, and Media

Discover how much the media (TV, movies, magazines, etc.) try to use sex to capture your attention. As teen and parent, read through a popular teen magazine or celebrity magazine and count how many times you can find a reference (in words or pictures) to sex, sensual clothing, physical attractiveness, etc. Discuss why they use sex in this way.

CHAPTER 19

HOW FAR?

Years ago, one of the guys in the youth group asked me a very important question. Denny had a girlfriend and needed help.

"She is so hot! How far can I go and still not be sinning?"

I knew Denny well enough to know that he was very serious about his question, and it demanded a careful answer. "Denny, do your parents have rules?"

"Yeah, I am afraid they do."

"Why do they have them?"

"To hassle us and yell at us."

"Seriously."

"To protect us and to help us to know what to do."

"Do they have rules just to be mean?" I continued.

"Some days it seems that way, but honestly, no."

"We have rules at our house too. We love our daughters, Brooke and Nicole, and we have rules to protect them from harm. The rules aren't bad, but the world is. Some people say the world is good and the rules are bad, but the opposite is true. The world is an evil place, and we can get hurt if we don't follow God's rules."

"So, what does God say? 'Thou shall not make out'? Or does He say anything at all?"

Denny wouldn't settle for simple answers.

"Well, God doesn't come right out and tell us all the details, but He does give us some principles as guidelines."

"What are they? And don't tell me no kissing until marriage," Denny insisted.

"God made sex for marriage. Listen to this verse: 'Marriage should be honored by all, and the marriage bed kept pure, for God will judge the adulterer and all the sexually immoral' (Heb. 13:4).

"So obviously sex before marriage is a definite no-no," I continued. "But what about all the other things, other than sexual intercourse? God will judge those who sin sexually. He does not want us to be impure." I paused to see if Denny was following what I was saying.

"Got it. Go on," he encouraged.

"The big question is, where do you draw the line? I think it has a lot to do with the individual."

"I agree," Denny said, nodding. "Some guys can't even hold a girl's hand without having intense hormone problems!"

We laughed, and I continued. "The Bible emphasizes purity, not any specific physical act. For some people, holding hands is the limit, because anything more would cause them to lust (want each other sexually). In other words, what goes on in your mind is just as important as what your hands do. One Scripture verse that I like on this topic of purity is:

> Don't let anyone look down on you because you are young,
> but set an example for the believers in speech, in life, in
> love, in faith and in purity (1 Tim. 4:12).

I continued my explanation. "So it's not just one thing; your whole lifestyle matters. You don't want to do anything or say anything that might cause people to doubt that you are a believer. In other words, if most of the guys at your school are making out with their girlfriends and you do the exact same thing, they won't know the difference between you and those who don't believe in Jesus. There should be some kind of difference. Christians need to have an observable higher standard."

"Do I have to be weird about it? Like never holding hands in public and always double dating?"

"No."

"Good. How do I set and keep higher standards? Give me an example."

"Your friends need to see your commitment to purity. It's a total commitment. Not just what you don't do (or do), but who you *are*. If they can see your commitment to purity, it will provide an example for them. Too many kids don't have standards. They let everyone else tell them what's right. That's not leading—that's following. Last I checked, there are plenty of followers but a shortage of leaders. God wants us to be this kind of leader in our relationships with the opposite sex. He wants us to be examples of purity."

I wasn't sure if I had done a good job of explaining this to Denny, so I asked him, "How far do you think you can go and still keep your purity?"

He responded with an intelligent answer. "Not far! But you should consider how old the people are, how long they have gone with each other, and how much self-control they have. It will take a lot of self-control to stay pure."

"Wow, that's great! You have really thought this topic through. Remember, Denny, the goal isn't to see how close you can get to sexual intercourse but to learn how you can protect something precious—your purity—and to honor God in all that you do."

"Yeah, I know. But are there *any* specific guidelines you can give me?"

Denny didn't settle for simple answers.

These are a few ideas I gave him to start with:

1. Hand-holding and sitting close to each other can be great ways to enjoy each other without getting yourselves into a bad situation.

2. Kissing on the lips on the first date is premature, and kisses that take a long time will just get you into trouble. Don't expect a kiss or a *feel* as repayment for a hamburger and a movie.

3. Don't lie down beside each other, especially if all you have on are your swimsuits. The temptation is just too strong.

4. Caressing or touching each other on the breasts and in the genital area is one guaranteed way to lose control. This is actually foreplay and is God's design for marriage to prepare married couples for sexual intercourse. Avoid this because it stimulates a desire that is designed to be met in marriage.

5. Don't be alone with your girlfriend in her home (or yours) when parents aren't there. No sitting on laps or sitting together in a parked car. These are situations where your impulses can drive you farther than your godly intentions.

Denny smiled at me, "Thanks Tim. This was really messing with my head. Now I know what to do."

Response

1. Can you express love in ways that aren't physical or sexual? How?
2. How do guidelines and rules protect us in life? Give examples.
3. When do sexual thoughts become impure?
4. What do you think about Tim's five guidelines he gave Denny?
5. Take another look at 1 Timothy 4:12 (on page 115). What do you think it means to be an example in each of these: speech, life, love, faith, and purity?

A Letter To My Son

Dear Son,

Sex. I know some people think that it is the last thing parents and teens should talk about. But it is too important to me to be sidetracked by news, weather, sports, or grades. This topic is an important one, even if it makes us uncomfortable

As you can see, I have talked with lots of teens like Denny. I want them to make wise decisions. I care about these teens, but not as much as I care for you! That's why we will talk about what it means to be man and woman. I want you too to make wise decisions in this area.

There are girls who are incredibly attractive and seductive; you could quickly find yourself caught up with one. For a close up look at how a woman seduces a man, read Proverbs 7. I remember discovering this chapter when I was in junior high Sunday School. Church was never so interesting!

Stay pure if you want to avoid the guilt and negative baggage that is involved with going too far sexually. Follow the five tips that I gave Denny.

With God's help you will be able to express your love to a girl in a fun and enjoyable way without it getting too hot and heavy.

Denny had the courage to bring up tough topics and still make it fun. You remind me of him.

Proudly,
Dad

"To live a life that is distinctive be committed to purity."—Dad

JOURNAL

Respond to the letter by writing your own thoughts here. Parents may want to use Tim's letter as a model for their own.

_____

_____

_____

_____

_____

_____

_____

_____

_____

➤ CONNECTION ◄

Watch a popular teen TV show. Record in writing how many times they make references to premarital sex. After watching the show discuss:

▶ Do I feel more or less pure after watching this TV show?

▶ What is this show trying to promote? What is the obvious message? What is the hidden message?

CHAPTER 20

TRUE LOVE WAITS

Believing that true love waits, I make a commitment to God, myself, my family, my friends, my future mate, and my future children to be sexually abstinent from this day until the day I enter a biblical marriage relationship.
—Signed by nearly a million
teenagers around the world.

T eens are having sex."

Don't buy the lie. Not all teens are having sex. They are seeing through our culture's deception and responding, "True love waits."

"Everybody's doing it" doesn't mean "I want to do it God's way."

"Let's prove our love" could also mean "Let's prove it by not having sex."

"You're hot!" doesn't mean "I love you for who you are."

"You are just what I need" doesn't mean "I will sacrifice to meet your needs."

"How could it be wrong, when it feels so right?" is just a lame excuse.

"I've got to have you" isn't the same as "I respect you enough to wait."

Sex is not the same as love no matter how much they sound the same.

Making love: It's in the movies, on TV, and splattered on the pages of magazines. I have never seen such an emphasis on pushing kids to be sexually active. You would think we would have learned something from the AIDS crisis and epidemic of sexually transmitted diseases.

Why do people think sex is such a big thing? It seems that having sex makes many teens feel as though they are mature; others do it to be popular or to be part of the in crowd. Some teens feel that everyone is doing it, and they don't want to be left out. Others have sex because it is fun. They say, "If it feels good, why not?"

But do these reasons really make sense? Will having sex make you more popular or give you true friendships?

By having sex before you are married, you are not showing your maturity; you are actually showing that you are immature, because you are doing something that God forbids. God tells us the only way to be prepared for sex is to make the commitments that are made in a wedding ceremony. There is a lot to know and think about before you say yes to having sex:

> God wants you to be holy, so you should keep clear of all sexual sin. Then each of you will . . . live in holiness and honor (1 Thes. 4:3-4, NLT).

Being pure in our sexual behavior is a characteristic of genuine Christians. There are other verses you can look at to see that God has designed sex for marriage. But let me give you some more reasons to remain a virgin in addition to the most important one: because God says to.

TEN REASONS TO REMAIN A VIRGIN UNTIL YOU ARE MARRIED

1. To protect yourself from making the physical and sexual part of life too big a deal. This part of life can easily begin to control us and cause us great pain and grief.

2. To protect yourself from distrust in marriage. If you give in to the sex pull now, you will live with the question in your mind, *Will I be able to control my sex life when I am married?* It is a painful and awkward spot to be in when you look at your wife on your wedding night and say, "Honey, I give you myself, but you aren't the first."

3. To protect yourself from guilt and anger. If you avoid having sex while you are unmarried, you will save yourself a truckload of guilt and a boxcar of anger. Sexually active relationships outside of marriage increase the potential of a broken relationship leaving both people feeling hurt, angry, and guilty.

4. To protect yourself from low self-esteem. Teens I know who have

had premarital sex have a lower view of themselves because they gave in to sexual temptation.

5. To avoid an unwanted pregnancy. Unless you are ready to be a daddy, stay away from sex!

6. To protect yourself from medical problems such as sexually transmitted diseases. In addition to AIDS, there are other diseases that can be very painful and damaging.

7. To protect yourself from emotional problems like depression.

8. To protect yourself from a perverted or depraved mind (see Romans 1). Playing around with sex can make you really obsessed with it.

9. To protect you from a cold conscience. If you are willing to ignore God's truth in this area of your life, you probably will become quite hard in other areas as well. This can lead to a real callousness toward God and His Word.

10. To protect yourself from sexual confusion and homosexuality. People who experiment with sex early often have bad experiences. These negative early experiences can cause strong negative images, leaving some teens repelled at the thought of having sex with someone of the opposite sex.

Probably one of the strongest arguments to avoid premarital sex is to preserve your innocence. As a teenager, you are caught in the middle; you aren't an adult and you aren't a child. In some ways, you are in a neutral zone between childhood and adulthood. This used to be a protected zone. Teens were once protected from the harsh realities of life, but now our culture rushes teens into "the real world" thinking we are preparing them for adulthood. Our culture has promoted a loss of innocence among teens, believing it's a sort of favor.

Teens have lost the safety and protection that comes from preserving adolescence as a stage of childhood. Teens miss out on that protected season that permits them to be progressively exposed to more adult situations. Instead, they get a truckload of information and experiences dumped on them all at once. For many teens, it is too much.

Protect your own innocence by avoiding premarital sex. You may be teased for it, but you will be saving the treasure of your innocence, a fortune that cannot be retrieved once it has been lost.

"Teens often mistake sex for love and fondling for affection."

RESPONSE

1. Where have you seen pressure for teens to have sex?

2. What are some reasons people make to encourage teens to have sex?

3. According to 1 Thessalonians 4:3-4 we are to "keep clear of all sexual sin" so we can be holy and pure. What does this mean to you? What does this look like for a teen? For a parent?

4. Take another look at the Ten Reasons to Remain a Virgin Until You Are Married. Which do you think is the strongest argument? The weakest? Do you have other reasons to add to the list?

5. Do you think teenagers have experienced a loss of innocence? Why do you think innocence is compared to treasure?

A LETTER TO MY SON

Dear Son,

I know everyone is pressured to be sexually active. Some people *expect* teens to be sexually active. But as you know, God doesn't expect us to be. He expects us to be pure, to maintain our sexual innocence until marriage. I have offered ten reasons why, but probably the one at the core of the issue has to do with passion. When we have our heart set on things that please God, it is easier to obey Him. If we compromise our hearts, it is much more difficult to do what He wants.

Let's say a Christian guy wants to grow in his relationship with God, but he and his girlfriend are tempted to go all the way. If he sets his heart on the natural passion, he may find himself being sexually active. But if he keeps his passion for God as his number one priority, he will be able to maintain his purity. There is a strong connection between passion and purity.

I have heard many teens admit, "I have lost my passion for God."

My response is often, "When did you become sexually active?"

They are surprised by my question and some are offended. They didn't expect their passion for God to relate to their sex life, but it does. God made us with a capacity to be very committed to what we are passionate about. Athletes and musicians will suffer blood, sweat, and tears because they are passionate about improving their skills.

Proverbs 4:23 reminds us to "Guard your heart, for it affects everything you do" (NLT). Be encouraged that God never asks you to do anything that He won't help you with. When you guard your heart, you guard your innocence. You don't let just any information or experience infiltrate your heart—you guard it. With a guarded heart, you will have a passion to be close to God and to do what He says. Then you will be enjoying life and living it in harmony with His design.

> Love,
> Dad

JOURNAL

Respond to the letter by writing your own thoughts here. Parents may want to use Tim's letter as a model for their own.

_____

_____

_____

_____

_____

_____

_____

_____

_____

◆ CONNECTION ◆

Make an "I'll Wait" covenant (like the one on page 119) that is a personal promise between you and God to maintain your sexual purity for marriage. Include 1 Thessalonians 4:3-4 or other Scripture passages. Consider making it look like a legal document by printing it on parchment paper and adding silver or gold stickers (available at office supply stores). The teen will make the covenant and the parent can design a ceremony that would be meaningful. Ceremonies might include:

▶ A special candlelit dinner at home with the teen's favorite food (siblings presence optional).

▶ An overnight to the mountains, beach, or lake to present the covenant.

▶ Going out to eat, just teen and parent(s), and then presenting the covenant back at home. (It's better to not do it at the restaurant.) Serve your favorite dessert.

CHAPTER 21

WHAT TO LOOK FOR
IN A WOMAN

It may have been the least popular talk I offered the guys in the youth group. We were talking about dating and relating to the opposite sex.

"How are we supposed to treat girls?" Chris asked.

"With respect and honor. We should treat them better than guys do who aren't believers. We have a higher standard," I explained.

"Higher standard? Is this high jumping or dating?"

"We should treat girls like our sisters."

"You mean, tease them and make fun of them?"

"No, treat them with sensitivity and care. We should remember that they are our sisters in Christ. We have the same Father who expects us to show kindness to each other."

You could feel the enthusiasm suck out of the room. My last few comments were as popular as day-old oatmeal. The guys liked the fantasy of romance. They didn't like the *family of God* idea. But I continued, "The Bible says we are to treat younger women as sisters, with absolute purity (1 Timothy 5:2). That means that we need to treat a girl with purity as you would your sister. She is your sister in Christ."

Their faces contorted as they considered this strange idea.

"Yeah," responded Rob. "I heard one guy say, 'Treat the girl you are going out with like you want some other guy to treat your future wife.'"

"Huh?"

"It means to treat girls the way you want your future wife to be treated," explained Rob.

"Wow! That sure puts a different twist on things!" exclaimed Chris. "Does that mean we can't kiss them or anything?"

"No, it just means to remember who their Dad is. As a sister in Christ, her Dad is God. He sees all, knows all, and is everywhere. And you are dating His daughter!"

"Oooh, that's kind of scary."

"Depends on what you are doing."

"Does that mean that we should only date Christian girls?"

"The Bible doesn't give dating tips, but it does warn us about being in partnership with unbelievers. Picture two oxen yoked together: one wants to go left and the other wants to go right. Scripture says, 'Do not be yoked together with unbelievers. For what do righteousness and wickedness have in common? Or what fellowship can light have with darkness? . . . What does a believer have in common with an unbeliever?' (2 Cor. 6:14-15). If you are going out with a non-Christian girl, she may want you to go left, but you need to go right. There will be tension. You are yoked with someone heading in a different direction. Next thing you know, you compromise your beliefs. Compromise comes easily when your heart is divided."

"Can't you go out without being 'yoked'?"

"Yeah, I suppose you could, but it's dangerous. Who is to say that you won't fall for this girl on your first date? You could be hopelessly in love after one movie and a bag of popcorn!"

"Okay. We should look for a Christian girl and treat her with purity and respect, like a sister. We should help each other stick to our standards. What else should we look for in a woman?" asked Steve.

"Yeah babee, we've graduated from girls to *women!*"

"Well, I am a senior . . . *boys,*" Steve asserted as he pointed to his chest.

"You want a WOG," I said.

"A hog?"

"No, a W.O.G.—a Woman of God. That is what you want, not just some babe. External beauty may fade. Go for the stuff that lasts. Listen to this: 'Charm is deceptive, and beauty is fleeting; but a woman who fears the Lord is to be praised' (Prov. 31:30)."

"WOG?"

I explained further. "You could be dating the most gorgeous girl at your school, but her looks may be temporary. Some women get prettier with age and others—well, let's say they lose it. The same goes for men. I went to my twenty-year high school reunion and noticed that some of the best looking girls in high school didn't look so hot now. And some of the 'plain Janes' had turned into super models! Beauty can change, so you need to look beyond a girl's looks to see her heart. Is she is kind? Does she have a heart for God? A woman with a heart for God is a WOG. Got it?"

"Got it!" echoed the guys.

RESPONSE

1. What are some ways a guy can show respect and honor to a girl?
2. What do you think about the concept of considering girls as sisters in Christ?
3. When would you say someone becomes yoked with another person?
4. What are some qualities of a woman who fears the Lord?
5. What are some of the qualities you find attractive in a girl?

A LETTER TO MY SON

Dear Son,

It's easy for us males to get hung up on beauty. We spend much of our time looking for, looking at, and dreaming about gorgeous babes. But we need to watch out for falling for the deception of beauty. It can be an incomplete picture. The girl you are first attracted to may have the qualities you want, or she may turn out to be less than you imagined. Her friend, standing next to her, may be overlooked at first glance, but she might actually be the in-depth beauty. Don't let the flashy one keep you from getting to know the true beauty.

Women are intriguing and fascinating. It takes time to discover what it is about them that we find attractive. That's why a lifetime of marriage is the way to go. It gives you plenty of time and the stability you want to pursue understanding the object of your love.

It has been my prayer, since you were born, that you would pursue a relationship with a wise young woman—a WOG. I got this idea from Proverbs where it talks about wisdom, comparing it to a righteous woman:

Blessed is the man who finds wisdom, the man who gains understanding.

For she is more profitable than silver and yields better returns than gold.

She is more precious than rubies; nothing you desire can compare with her.

Long life is in her right hand; in her left hand are riches and honor.

Her ways are pleasant ways and all her paths are peace.

She is a tree of life to those who embrace her; those who lay hold of her will be blessed (Prov. 3:13-18).

"Nothing you desire can compare with a woman of God."
Not beauty.
Not riches.
Not power.
Not fame.
Nothing.
A woman of God is a true treasure. Seek her with all your heart.

Son, it has been my privilege to talk to hundreds of teens about what to look for in a woman or a man. I like to remind them that dating is preparation for marriage. Not everyone you go out with will be someone you would want to marry. But dating is good preparation for marriage because it helps you learn about qualities you want in a marriage partner. You also discover how to relate to women in a variety of settings. Dating can teach you some important things about yourself and how to get along with women. These insights should help you honor and respect women.

Here is my checklist to know if you are in a healthy relationship with a girl. It spells the word **HEALTH**:

▶ Honest. Is your relationship open and honest? Can you be transparent with each other? Are there any secrets you are hiding from her?

▶ Encourage. Does she encourage you? Has your faith been stronger as a result of being with her? Do you have more confidence as a result of her?

▶ Accepting. A healthy relationship accepts each other, with all of the strengths and weaknesses. An unhealthy relationship is one that is becoming more critical and negative.

▶ **L**ike. Do you like your girlfriend? I know that sounds funny, but do you enjoy spending time with her, or do you do it because you have to? Are you comfortable with her? Do you relax with her? Do you like how you feel when you are with her?

▶ **T**rust. Are you growing to trust each other more? An unhealthy relationship is marked my suspicion and jealously. Trust leads to freedom and security.

▶ **H**oly. Are you staying pure? As a result of being together, are you both becoming more like Christ? Are you growing in your faith, or has it become stagnant or slipped backwards?

There you have it—six indicators to check and see if your relationship with a girl is healthy.

I hope they prove to be helpful.

Love,
Dad

JOURNAL

Respond to the letter by writing your own thoughts in the section below. Parents may want to use Tim's letter as a model for their own.

_____

_____

_____

_____

_____

_____

_____

_____

➡ CONNECTION ⬅

Qualities I Like	**Qualities I Dislike**
_____	_____
_____	_____
_____	_____
_____	_____
_____	_____
_____	_____
_____	_____
_____	_____

1. List the qualities you like and dislike in a person of the opposite sex.

2. Put a question mark (?) by the qualities you dislike so much that you would have a hard time living with the person who had them.

3. Put an exclamation point (!) by the qualities you like and would really want in a woman.

4. Discuss with your parent or teen what you wrote.

5. Teens: What first attracted your parent(s) to his or her spouse? Ask them to describe the qualities that first drew them into the relationship.

CHAPTER *22*

READY TO DATE?

Lisa was a model Christian. In seventh grade she was the first to raise her hand and answer a question in Sunday School—but that was about the only time she would talk. In eighth grade she opened up more, but she was still a little self-conscious. She was a few pounds overweight and in spite of her long, pretty hair and sparkling eyes, Lisa felt ugly. In ninth grade she grew a few inches and lost a few pounds. In tenth grade she was becoming one of the regulars at youth group and joined our student leadership team. As a junior, she was one of the most well-liked people in our group. At summer camp, before her senior year, she rededicated her life to God, including her dating life.

Eighteen months later, Lisa was depressed. She was angry and felt dirty and used. She was no longer a virgin. She was no longer a smiling, growing Christian.

What happened to Lisa?

Read the letter she wrote me.

LISA'S STORY

I think the last time I wrote you I was just starting a relationship with a non-Christian guy named "Bill." I remember I was having a lot of conflict in my heart with God and temptation. Well, since I wasn't too heavily involved with Christian fellowship, I ended up giving into temptation for the whole next year. Like they say, "I fell totally!" I did everything I thought I'd never do, and I tried everything once. BUT . . . I got it all out of my system. We got engaged and I went away to college. It was really hard being away, but I really thought it was going to work. What I didn't realize was that there was no way I was going to give my life back to God as long as I was together with Bill, because he wasn't a Christian. I wasn't going to do anything that might break us up. Well, God took care of that situation real fast!

Two days after I came back at Christmas break, Bill broke up with me! The engagement was off. I knew that I shouldn't be making plans to marry a non-Christian. Tim, you taught us that! Maybe this was God's way of protecting me.

Now, I feel myself growing closer to God every day since we broke up. I know it's for the best. It's hard though, because I still am very much in love with Bill and it hurts to see his life so messed up. I feel the pain of how I disappointed God. I am praying for Bill, but I don't think he will listen to me now. I am not a very good example of a Christian.

Tim, thanks for your help. You'd think after all those talks and Bible studies in youth group that I would have known better than to fall for a non-Christian and become sexually involved. It's weird, because I really did know better. I knew I was on dangerous ground, but I did it anyway. Why do people do exactly the opposite of what they know is right?

Love,
Lisa

"Why do people do exactly the opposite of what they know is right?" Lisa's question is penetrating. How would you answer it? As I gave it some thought, it occurred to me that many times we follow advice on how to live from a dead man. We are getting our cues on dating from the wrong source.

As for you, you were dead in your transgressions and sins, in which you used to live when you followed the ways of this world and of the ruler of the kingdom of the air, the spirit who is now at work in those who are disobedient. All of us also lived among them at one time, gratifying the cravings of our sinful nature and following its desires and thoughts (Eph. 2:1-3).

As Christians, we shouldn't follow the *ways of this world* as if we were still *dead in our sin*. We need to shed the old sinful nature and its desires and thoughts and exchange it for a fresh and godly approach. In other words, Christians need to re-think dating and not simply follow the patterns of the world.

I could tell you stories of dozens of teens who, like Lisa, got trapped in the *ways of this world* when it came to dating. They wound up disobeying God and chased after their own desires. That is why *people do exactly the opposite of what they know is right.*

The world traps us into tragic dating by unleashing five snares that may look good at first, but that eventually snag us into pain, compromise, and confusion.

FIVE DATING TRAPS

1. The Trap of Sex

Lisa and Bill know the power of this trap. Sex is a powerful force. It can pull a husband and wife together, or it can blast apart a boyfriend and girlfriend. Our culture puts too much emphasis on sex. It's a *without-a-kiss-on-the-first-date-it's-a-waste* mentality. All of the statistics point to a rise on sexually transmitted diseases. Even with all of the condom education, more teens are coming home from a date with a sexual experience and a disease. Condoms certainly aren't the answer; abstinence is.

2. The Trap of Status Dating

I like to call this "date-to-rate." It's going out with a person because she makes you look better. This trap is dangerous because it is actually using a person. People who are into status dating are motivated by fear and peer pressure. They want to go out with someone, not because they actually like that person, but because she "looks good on them," kind of like a leather jacket. Status dating is based on ownership: "This is MY girlfriend." A status dater runs the risk of rejection by those he seeks to impress and his date. Especially when she finds out he is using her.

3. The Trap of the Perfect Mate

Dating can be tragic when you are looking for the perfect woman. I know high school students who are stressed about finding the ultimate mate. I tell them, "Lighten up! You are only fifteen." Dating is designed to help you understand women and yourself. It isn't simply a sorting process for you to get the *perfect match*. If you are out to "date-to-mate," you could be adding a lot of unnecessary stress in your life.

4. The Trap of Hyper Dating

Activity doesn't equal quality. Yet some teens get wrapped up in the activity and frequency of dating and forget to focus on the relationship. I call this "Disneyland Dating." It's lots of fun, fantasy, and activity, but it doesn't do much to deepen the relationship. If you become addicted to hyper dating you will miss out on the real thing—a deep, caring relationship. You will miss a genuine friendship with a girl, a friendship that doesn't need amusement to be satisfying.

5. The Trap of Different Directions

If you are going out with someone who doesn't share your faith, you are going in different directions. It's like kissing a passing train. It may be real, fun, and exciting, but you could easily be hurt. Going out with people who claim to be Christians, but who don't live up to God's standards, won't help you either. The real ticket is finding someone who is heading in the same direction as you are. With this kind of girl, you can share the most important things in life, such as your faith.

Another way you will experience conflict is if your age or interests or activities are really different. Let's say you graduated from high school and your girlfriend is in high school. This can add some stress to the relationship. You live in two different worlds.

READY TO DATE?

"When is a teen ready to date?" I wish I had a buck for every time I was asked this question. I would go out and buy myself a Porsche. A person isn't necessarily ready to date when he or she hits the magic age of sixteen. It's not an issue of age; it is an issue of preparation.

▶ A teen is ready to date when he knows the dangers of dating. We listed the five traps above.

▶ A teen is ready to date when he knows the benefits of dating. Do you know what they are?

▶ A teen is ready to date when he has written his Personal Dating Standards and is willing to stick to them.

It all adds up to this: *You are ready to date when you know the dangers and benefits of dating and have written your standards and are willing to commit to them.*

Lisa could have avoided all kinds of pain had she done this. To most people, she was old enough to date, but obviously *she wasn't prepared to date.*

RESPONSE

1. What do you think went wrong with Lisa?

2. How would you respond to Lisa's question: "Why do people do exactly the opposite of what they know is right?"

3. Which of the Five Dating Traps have you observed or experienced?

4. When, in your opinion, is someone ready to date?

5. What are some of the benefits, dangers, and standards for dating?

A LETTER TO MY SON

Dear Son,

Benefits, dangers, standards? It sounds more like life insurance than dating, doesn't it? I hope I didn't take the fun and anticipation out of dating for you. I actually believe that these suggestions will make dating more fun and protect you from harm. That's my job, you know: to guide you in life and protect you from getting hurt. And if I can add a little more fun, that is better yet!

I have shared these ideas with hundreds of teens. I have never had one come back to me and say this approach was a waste of time or that it didn't work. I have heard from dozens who have told me that they improved their dating by thinking through the benefits and dangers and making a personal commitment to standards. I have also seen too many teens make foolish decisions because they didn't have a dating game plan. They tried dating without considering the dangers and the benefits. They tried dating without a clear commitment to standards. In other words, they dated by "feel" not by thinking. When you let your feelings influence your dating, you are asking for trouble. Most of us need some guardrails to keep us on track. We can't expect our changing emotions to keep us on track.

Imagine you are driving on a winding mountain road that is slick with ice. The road is carved out of the side of a steep mountain cliff; inches from the road a cliff drops off two hundred feet straight down. You are glad to discover that some thoughtful highway engineer designed and built guardrails to keep you from plunging to your death. They are eighteen inches wide and painted bright yellow. They are supported by brown four-by-fours. You feel secure until a passenger shouts, " Slow down, this is too dangerous!"

"Don't worry. I can handle it."

"But the road is slippery and there's the cliff!"

"But we have these nice guardrails."

"You mean the ones made out of cardboard?"

Trusting in your feelings to guide and protect your dating life is like trusting in cardboard guardrails on an icy mountain road; they can't be relied upon!

That is why I want us to talk about the benefits and dangers of dating and to develop standards that will be yours to use in dating. I want to build something into your life that you can rely on.

Keeping my eyes on the road,
Dad

JOURNAL

Respond to the letter by writing your own thoughts here. Parents may want to use Tim's letter as a model for their own.

_____

_____

_____

_____

_____

_____

_____

_____

_____

▶ CONNECTION ◀

As parent and teen, list the benefits and dangers of dating. Don't look at each other's papers. When you are done, compare. Discuss how dating has changed from the time your mom or dad dated. Then see if you can come up with three possible dating standards. Try it separately first, then compare again. Then see if you can come up with four that you agree on (both parent and teen).

Rent a video that shows dating from years gone by. Have some popcorn and enjoy the contrast and similarities to today's dating. (Try *Gidget* movies; *Grease; Beach Blanket Bingo;* etc.)

CHAPTER 23

BEER PRESSURE

Brian is a hot surfer and a lot of fun. But when it comes to backbone, he has none. He used to come to youth group, but he started to hang out with some guys who liked to drink beer. They pressured Brian to join them. He eventually gave in.

One day they ran out of beer. The group elected Brian to steal some from the convenience store. He wanted to be accepted, so he gave in.

He stole a twelve-pack from the 7 Eleven. I'm not sure how you shoplift a twelve-pack, but Brian tried. He made his getaway. The only problem was, he was riding his bike!

Picture a sixteen year old tearing down the street with a twelve-pack of beer under his arm. The store clerk saw him steal the beer and called the police. The officer chased him down the streets of our neighborhood.

Brian tried to ditch the cop, but the cruiser was much faster than his rapidly pedaling legs. In desperation, Brian threw the beer in a ditch and tried to pedal faster. The cop warned him to pull over, but Brian ignored him and tried to get away. The cop swerved in front of Brian, knocking him off his bike. The cop caught him, handcuffed him, and put him in the back of the cruiser. He recovered the beer as evidence and hauled Brian off to jail.

Beer on a bike?

Brian suffered from *beer pressure.*

Brian gave in to his friends because he thought they would reject him if he didn't. When we give in to the demands of others, we lose control. Control of ourselves. Control of the situation. Control of the consequences.

Giving in to others' expectations leaves you with little influence. You go along for the ride, but you aren't driving.

Brian discovered his friends liked being in the driver's seat. Their "coolness" controlled his behavior. It made him do stupid things like steal-ing beer on a bike! His worst fear was that his friends would reject him. When they saw the lights on the police car, his so-called friends ditched him. His fears became reality.

Some *friends!*

We don't have to look far to see that each of us has a friend like Brian—someone who is easily influenced by peer pressure to abuse sub-stances like alcohol or drugs. In high school, I watched a friend destroy his life with substance abuse. I didn't know how to help him. I know more now. Here are some suggestions to help you help a friend who might be abusing drugs or alcohol.

TEN TIPS TO HELP A FRIEND

1. Decide which is more important: your friend liking you or doing what is best for him. If you want him to like you, and you really don't care about him and his health, then let it go—do nothing.

2. If you care about your friend, then let him know it. Say, "I like you. I'm glad we are friends."

3. At another time say, "I care about you and want you to know that I'm worried about you. I am concerned about your drinking (or drug abuse)."

4. Ask him why he drinks. Also ask if you can still be friends if you don't party with him.

5. If you are close friends, ask him to stop (or at least consider stop-ping as a favor to you). Pray for your friend to lose his desire for abusing substances.

6. If he ignores you, or is rude to you, talk to your parent, a youth worker, or an adult you trust. Ask for the adult's advice.

7. Be willing to do a little private-eye work to find out how often your friend abuses substances, where, with whom, and where he gets his drugs or alcohol.

8. After you have done your detective work, write down the infor-mation. Go to him and say, "I have told you I care about you, and I am still worried about your substance abuse. I know that you are using it on (time) with (persons) and where you get it. I really want you to consider

what you are doing to yourself. Remember I care about you. I want to see you get help."

9. Keep praying for him to feel convicted about his substance abuse. Also pray for another time to talk with him when he is serious and sober.

10. After a while if your friend doesn't quit or seek help, you have three options:

▶ Tell him you will go with him to get help.

▶ Tell him your friendship is over. You gave it your best shot.

▶ Get some help. Talk to his parents, a youth worker, a counselor, or teacher.

Sometimes the most helpful and loving thing you can do for a friend is get him in trouble. Actually, he is in trouble, and you are simply getting him in touch with someone who can help.

Sometimes I have found it helpful to say, "I have done all kinds of things to help you (remind him of the steps you took), but you just don't seem to care. I am angry and disappointed. This problem is bigger than you. You need help." Try not to say it in a critical or condemning way. Just state the facts and your feelings.

This is playing hardball, but for some, it is the only way. If you love a person, you will do what is best for him; even though he may hate you for it. This is what is called Tough Love, and it is needed if you are going to help someone with a substance abuse problem.

Review the ten tips again. I hope they seem useful. I have seen lots of teenagers mess up their lives with drugs and alcohol. I have also seen God use loving friends like you to reach out and help friends with a substance abuse problem. You may have to use this approach with a friend this year. Chances are, you will have a friend with this problem. Maybe you will know what to do. I didn't.

"Wounds from a friend are better than many kisses from an enemy" (Prov. 27:6, NLT).

RESPONSE

1. What do you think about the story about Brian?

2. Why do you think we sometimes allow ourselves to be controlled

by the expectations of others?

3. What do you think about the Ten Tips to Help a Friend? Which would be the most difficult for you to do?

4. Love must be tough. What do you think about the statement, "Love is doing what is best for the person?"

5. How can a *wound from a friend* be helpful? (Proverbs 27:6)

A LETTER TO MY SON

Dear Son,

You will encounter all kinds of opportunities to experiment with alcohol or drugs in the next few years. You may see some of your friends drastically change. For some, it will be tragic.

I wish I could keep you from the temptation and the pain. But I can't put you in a space station on Mars. All I can do is give you some tips about how to protect yourself and how to help a friend who might need it.

When it comes to substance abuse, or driving while under the influence, the best approach is tough love. The risks are too high to be *nice*. I know some kids who wished they weren't so nice; maybe their friends would still be alive. Be willing to love your friends enough to say, "Enough!" If you love a person, you will do what is best for him, even though that person may hate you for it.

Please feel free to come to me or Mom for help with these kinds of problems. I have seen too many kids try to deal with this by themselves. You don't have to handle it alone. I hope these ideas will help you know how to help a friend who may need it. Don't worry about doing it perfectly; it is better to try to help than to not help at all. After all, we are all learning to help; this kind of thing is new to all of us. Probably nobody will do it perfectly. That's not the point. The point is to care enough to confront. To care enough to take action. To care enough to say, "My friend matters."

I will be there for you.

Love, Dad

JOURNAL

Respond to the letter by writing your own thoughts in the section below. Parents may want to use Tim's letter as a model for their own.

_____

_____

_____

_____

_____

_____

_____

_____

▶ CONNECTION ◀

Develop a contract like the ones used by SADD (Students Against Driving Drunk*) between teen and parent that deals with substance abuse. Describe what you plan to do when faced with various situations. Try to be fair, neutral, realistic, and understanding.

Discuss, as parent and teen, how you plan to use the contract. Make a copy for both parent and teen. Discuss and revise every year.

----

*See Appendix A

CHAPTER 24

SUPERNATURAL ENCOUNTERS

A liens Abducted Me"
    "Meet Your Spirit Guide"
    "Enhance Your Cosmic Power"
"Discover Your Former Self"
"Communicate with Dead Loved Ones"

These aren't simply headlines from a tabloid. These are ads found in popular magazines and newspapers. We are in an age interested in the supernatural. A few years ago, angels were quite the rage. We saw all kinds of angel books, pins, clothing, decorating items, screen savers, and testimonials on talk shows about "angel encounters."

Isn't this interest in the supernatural good?

"Get answers on life, love, and your future! Call Psychic Friends Hotline to find out if she really does like you, before you make a major decision or invest your money. Your happiness and taking control over your life are important to your friends at the Psychic Friends Hotline. Call now."

Contrast the ads and the talk shows with the following Scripture passage:

> Let no one be found among you who sacrifices his son or daughter in the fire, who practices divination or sorcery, interprets omens, engages in witchcraft, or cast spells, or who is a medium or spiritist or who consults the dead. Anyone who does these things is detestable to the LORD, and because of these detestable practices the LORD your God will drive out those nations before you. You must be blameless before the LORD your God. (Deut. 18:10-13).

God doesn't cut us any slack when it comes to messing with the dark side of the supernatural. He says, "Don't!" In case you have any question, He clears it up with the last line, "You must be blameless before the Lord your God." In other words, steer clear of anything that is supernatural that isn't from God. Chances are, it is evil.

But our culture's fascination with psychics and other forms of the supernatural seems to be growing. Why is that?

Human beings are spiritual creatures. We look for an encounter with the spiritual. We instinctively know that life is beyond what we experience naturally with our five senses. We have a built-in hunger for the supernatural. We want to find out what is beyond our routine existence. For some, this includes a voyage into the occult.

The word occult means the *practice of studying the supernatural, or some secret knowledge of supernormal powers.* The following list will help you see the occult's influence in our world. Consider how interest in each has increased in recent years:

▶ Psychics
▶ Vampires
▶ Witches and wicca
▶ Séances
▶ Spirit guides
▶ Channeling
▶ Crystals
▶ UFOs
▶ Ouija boards
▶ Fantasy games
▶ Satanism
▶ Music promoting satanism
▶ Paganism
▶ New age philosophies
▶ Astrology

We don't have the time to deal with all of these issues, but they are all evidence of increasing fascination with the occult.

THE SOURCE

Satan, God's enemy is the source behind all occult activity. He is alive and well, and he seeks to destroy all who come up against him. Satan is a real, supernatural being, not that cute, horned guy in the red pajamas. He is real and presents himself as an angel of light. He has been called the great deceiver. One of his strategies is to convince us that the Bible has gone out of style and that there are newer and more sophisticated truths that can lead us to a higher plane of fulfillment and enlightenment.

Satan was once a high-ranking angel named Lucifer who rebelled against God and took a third of the angels with him. We call these fallen angels demons. Since they are spiritual beings, they have spiritual powers. They aren't limited physically like we are. As a result, they can do all kinds of magic.

The Bible warns us of this:

> The coming of the lawless one will be in accordance with the work of Satan displayed in all kinds of counterfeit miracles, signs and wonders, and in every sort of evil that deceives those who are perishing. They perish because they have refused to love the truth and so be saved. For this reason God sends them a powerful delusion so they will believe the lie (2 Thes. 2:9-11).

All around us we see proof that people have "believed the lie." They have been deceived. Satan lied to Adam and Eve: "Eat the fruit and you will be like God," he enticed. It's the same old lie, but now he puts a modern twist on it.

What should our response be?

Fascinated or afraid? No, we should be alert and aware.

Consider what Scripture says about our enemy:

> Be self-controlled and alert. Your enemy the devil prowls around like a roaring lion looking for someone to devour. Resist him, standing firm in the faith, because you know that your brothers throughout the world are undergoing the same kind of sufferings (1 Peter 5:8-9).

It's not enough to ignore our enemy; we need to defend against him. He will attack us. We will need to be alert and ready to stand our ground. One way to fight against him is to understand his weapons. If we understand the enemy's weapons, we can strategize against them.

LIES

One of Satan's most often-used weapons is deception. Jesus called him "the father of lies." Satan is an expert liar; it is his first language. He has three favorite lies that he has been using since he deceived Adam and Eve in the Garden:

1. Christ is not God's only Son—there are other teachers and angels equal to Him.

2. There are many paths to peace with God, so Christ's death on the cross wasn't really necessary.

3. We all have within us the innate power to become like God, if only we would learn how to unleash it.[1]

POWERS

Another weapon that Satan uses is his appeal to us to use supernatural powers. This is easily seen in the recent increase in fascination of witchcraft or wicca. Wicca means *to bend or alter shape.* It comes from the same idea as wicker furniture (you know, the kind that is bent into shapes and twisted together). Witchcraft is the *twisting* of the truth to show off some kind of power. Hexes, curses, spells, and portents all refer to using witchcraft, *white* magic, sorcery, or shamanism.

Young people who feel weak or ignored are often drawn to this kind of dark power. They seek to have influence over others. Some seek revenge against those who have hurt them.

Fantasy games, certain card games, and TV (for instance *Charmed* and *Sabrina: the Teenage Witch*) all promote the casting of hexes and spells. How can we know if something is dangerous?

TEST THE SPIRITS

Scripture tells us "do not believe every spirit, but test the spirits to see whether they are from God, because many false prophets have gone into the world" (1 John 4:1). Can you discern the difference between a real messenger from God and a fake one?

A real messenger from God:

1. Claims that Jesus is God's Son—fully human, fully God.

2. Calls attention to Christ (not himself) and to the work of salvation He completed on the cross.

3. Elevates Scripture as the final authority for evaluating truth.

4. Never encourages being involved in the occult.

If a psychic on TV claims to have "special knowledge," evaluate his or her claim against this test. If a friend wants to play a computer fantasy game that evokes "powers, forces, and spells from the ancient seers," use this test to determine the spirit behind the game. It may be an evil spirit.

RESPONSE

1. Study the fifteen occult influences on page 144. Have you seen an increase in some of these? Describe your observation.

2. What are some ways Satan deceives?

3. How can we be alert without being obsessed with Satan's strategies?

4. Evaluate the fifteen occultic practices against Satan's three lies on page 146.

5. Use the four points of Test The Spirits above to evaluate some of the fifteen occultic practices. Choose those with which you are most familiar.

A LETTER TO MY SON

Dear Son,

The idea that we have an Enemy that seeks to destroy us isn't a pleasant topic, but it is true. I hope that you will be alert to the sneaky ways Satan tries to deceive, distract, and destroy.

You will have opportunities to get involved in some of this stuff. Your friend might get a cool video game that is a hot, first person shooter (FPS) game with all kinds of powerful automatic weapons. "Blast away with the new *Dungeons of Molech Version 3,* with state-of-the-art graphics, animation, and sound."

Others may tease you, "Come on! It's only five dollars for five minutes. What could be harmful? Let's have fun and call our Psychic Friends."

Or, "What harm can a TV show be that is obviously make-believe? Do you really think this witch stuff is real? It is so obvious that it is just Hollywood."

What will you do in those situations? Are you prepared to deal with them? I hope that you turn to your best weapon: God's Word. It is your sword in battle against the deceiver. Take time to read the verses in this chapter. Let them soak into your soul. They will protect you and give you the ability to fight back in spiritual warfare. It's not a fight we can handle with physical tools. It requires an arsenal of spiritual weapons. As you prepare for spiritual battle, your discernment into spiritual matters will increase. You will gain a clearer understanding of what is going on at a deeper level. You will be alert to the schemes of the evil one.

You will then be prepared.

> Victory is certain,
> Dad

➡ CONNECTION ⬅

Make a list of the fifteen practices of the occult from page 144. Get a large piece of poster board (11" x 17" or bigger). Look for examples of the fifteen practices in magazines, ads, and newspapers. You may also look on TV. Try to get at least one example for each. Glue the clipping on the poster board or describe in words an example of each.

Read and discuss Deuteronomy 18:10 and decide how you might represent this Scripture verse on your poster.

---

1 Bill Myers and David Wimbish, *The Dark Side of the Supernatural* (Minneapolis, MN: Bethany House Publishers, 1999), 20; Adapted.

CHAPTER 25

MUSIC MANIA

I wish I had a dollar for every time I have been asked, "Should a Christian listen to secular music?" I would have enough money to buy a very powerful stereo for my car! I get this question from parents and teens. It can be a hot issue. Some people are convinced that all rock music is "a tool of the Devil." Other people use contemporary music to reach people and preach the Gospel.

So why all the fuss? Why are so many people fighting over music? What's with all the music mania?

I believe that popular music (all forms) can be helpful or it can be destructive. The key is to evaluate your music.

Most teens like some form of popular music: hip hop, rap, rock, alternative, Goth, metal, techno, or whatever you are into. Usually, you like the same music your friends do. Not to like popular music is like trying to be unpopular. It's like saying, "I am trying to be a social loser."

But let's take a closer look. Forget about how popular your form of music is, and ask yourself, *What do I like about this music?* Is it the lyrics, the artist's talent, the band's look, the beat, or what? Sometimes we listen to popular music just because "everyone else does."

I remember hearing a song on the radio while I was driving a bus full of middle school students. I thought the song was terrible. It was boring, the guy sang off-key, and the rhythm was really weak. I thought it stunk!

But the kids loved it! They said, "That's such a hot hit!"

I wonder if everyone on that bus really liked the song, or if peer pressure forced some people to say that they liked the song, when they were really thinking, *This song really stinks, but everyone else likes it, so I will pretend to too.*

It makes me wonder how many bad songs become hits because of this jump-on-the-bandwagon mentality.

The problem begins when a popular song talks about doing things that go against what the Bible says or what a Christian believes. I am not saying, "Listen only to church organ and bell music." But we should think about the music we listen to and buy.

To help you evaluate your music, use the **B.E.S.T**. method for evaluating music:

BUILD: Does this music *build* me up and make me a better person and stronger Christian? The things that build up are those that help make me a servant and lead to unity.

ENCOURAGE: Does my music *encourage* others and me, or does it lead to discouragement and frustration? I believe it is wrong for Christians to do anything that discourages others from knowing God or being excited about all the good things God has done for us.

"So then, let us aim for harmony in the church and try to build each other up" (Rom. 14:19, NLT).

Try an experiment: listen to your favorite music for thirty minutes, then ask yourself, *Do I feel more encouraged? Do I have more courage to do what I should do?*

It's difficult for Christian teens to be really encouraged by music that has lyrics that go against God. That is why some popular music leads to a kind of war inside the Christian teen. There is no peace inside because the message of the song doesn't fit with God, who lives inside the Christian teen.

STUMBLE: Does my music cause me, or others to *stumble* or trip when it comes to understanding God or a relationship with Him?

> Decide instead to live in such a way that you will not put an obstacle in another Christian's path. . . . Don't eat meat or drink wine or do anything else if it might cause another Christian to stumble (Rom. 14:13, 21, NLT).

Would others have questions about your faith if they heard you listening to your music? Would they ask, "What is a Christian doing listening to music like that?" If something we do causes someone to criticize Christians, or if it confuses them about what a Christian is, then we should ask ourselves if we really have the freedom to be involved in that activity.

If people look at our music, and they see nothing different from teens who do not know God, then something is wrong. We have become exactly like the world. Instead, people should be able to see the distinctive difference that God makes in the lives of teens who know Him.

TELL: Does my music *tell* about my relationship with God and all the great things He has done for the world and me? Does it make God look good, or does it call attention to me? Sometimes we listen to music because we want others to notice us. "Hey, look at the dude with the crankin' stereo and the hot tunes!"

As Christians, it is our job to make God look good. The Bible calls this glorifying God. It means to put the spotlight on God and call attention to who He is and what He has done for us.

First Corinthians 10:31 reminds us: "Whatever you eat or drink or whatever you do, you must do all for the glory of God" (NLT).

One of the *best* ways to glorify God is to listen to contemporary Christian music. There are all kinds of styles: rap, hip hop, metal, pop, dance, alternative, country, folk, Goth, you name it. If they play it on the radio, you can find a Christian band that sounds similar. A lot of these groups make music that passes the **B.E.S.T.** test. Check it out. Contrast a popular secular group with a contemporary Christian group using the **B.E.S.T.** standard.

Music can influence us in huge ways, so let's make sure that it takes us in the right direction.

RESPONSE

1. Ask your parent to share a story about how popular music was considered bad in "the old days" (when he or she was a teenager).

2. Try to guess your parent's (or teen's) favorite music and artist.

3. Take another look at the **B.E.S.T.** method of evaluating music on pages 150-151. What do you think about this approach?

4. The third letter, S, stands for stumble. Why should we care if our music causes someone to stumble? Can't we listen to it if we like it?

5. See if you can trade stories about how God uses music to reach people.

A LETTER TO MY SON

Dear Son,

I know how much you like music; I hear it pounding constantly in your room! You like to punch in your favorite radio station when we are riding in the car. You feel it's important to listen to the "right" station and the "right" song and listen to it LOUD! (Especially if your friends are riding with us.)

There is one issue I would like to focus on, and it is different from evaluating music. Sure, I want you to evaluate your music so you purchase CDs and listen to songs that will help you, not hurt you.

Music is incredibly powerful. God made it that way. Here is what I want you to think about, something more positive than evaluating your music. *Sing to the Lord.*

Yup, that's it, *Sing to the Lord.*

It's really important. It's not just for choirs, angels, and squeaky-clean altar boys; it's for everybody. *Sing to the Lord.*

When you get up in the morning.
Sing to the Lord.
When you walk to class.
Sing to the Lord. (Or hum)
When you play ball.
Sing to the Lord.
When you do homework.
Sing to the Lord.
When you relax.
Sing to the Lord.
When you go to sleep.
Sing to the Lord.

If you do this, it will positively impact your day.

"Come, let us sing for joy to the LORD; let us shout aloud to the Rock of our salvation. Let us come before him with thanksgiving and extol him with music and song" (Ps. 95:1-2).

When we take time to praise God with singing, it changes us. It gives us a fresh perspective and gets our eyes off ourselves. It makes us thankful. So the next time you are feeling sad for yourself: *SING TO THE LORD!*

Singing with you,
Dad

JOURNAL

Respond to the letter by writing your own thoughts here. Parents may want to use Tim's letter as a model for their own.

_____

_____

_____

_____

_____

_____

_____

_____

_____

➡ CONNECTION ⬅

Go to a Christian concert together (teen and parent). I suggest you let the teen choose the concert.

Option A: Spend a few hours listening to contemporary Christian music at a bookstore that has listening stations. Try to find a new artist that you like.

Option B: Play your favorite music for each other (parent and teen). Then discuss why you like it.

CHAPTER 26

GIVE A LIFE

Think of your life as a house. Which rooms are off limits to God? You might feel as if you would lose some fun if you let God into your recreation room. How about your bedroom? *I wonder if God would like my magazines, posters, and music?*

What would God say about the garage? *Oh no! God will make me drive more slowly if I let Him in there!*

See what I mean? What areas of life are closed rooms to God? Sure, there is the living room. That is the showcase—the room where everything is perfect because no one is allowed to live in there! Some people are like that with God. *Keep Him in the living room, right out in front, for everyone to see. But don't let Him go snooping into the rest of my house. Keep Him in that one place.*

This kind of keep-God-in-the-living-room mentality is called compartmentalizing. Big word, huh? It means keeping God in some compartments of my life and not allowing Him into others. It means thinking about God at church but not at school. It means singing praises at youth group and swearing at soccer practice. This approach produces a wimpy faith, a fake faith. When we decide to let God into every area of our life, our faith is strengthened. It forces our faith to become real.

CHUCK'S WORLD

Chuck was a star tackle on his high school football team. One Sunday, I taught a lesson about including God in everything you do and giving Him the credit.

Chuck came up after class and asked, "You mean I can rip the heads off running backs and give God the credit?"

"Yeah Chuck. God has given you strength, size, and skill. Use your talent to the best of your abilities and give God the credit."

His eyes lit up because he had just been given permission to do what he loved to do. That Friday, he went out and played his best game. Afterward, a reporter from the local TV station interviewed him.

"Chuck, you played an outstanding game. Congratulations."

"Thanks. I want to give credit to God who gave me health and strength. I play the best I can to please Him. He's the coach in the sky."

Chuck continued to play well and won a scholarship to a university. He took every opportunity he had to call attention to Jesus. He even started a Bible study for the players and led it for four years. It was well attended, but then who was going to say no to Chuck?

YOUR REPUTATION

"If you don't stand for something, you will fall for anything." What are you willing to stand for? At your high school ten-year reunion, what do you want people to say about you?

"He's not so fat."

"He's kept most of his hair."

Or, "He still stands up for Christ."

"What are you standing for at your high school campus?" These were my words to challenge the high school students in our youth group. I had observed students who came to youth group and acted like Christians but who acted quite differently at school.

"Sometimes kids will tease you at school if you stand up for what you believe. Being a Christian doesn't mean your life will be easy. God doesn't push the delete button on all your problems when you become a Christian. Sometimes being a Christian *creates* problems. What it comes down to are two questions: Are you more concerned about what *they* think? Or are you more concerned about what God thinks? Are you a people-pleaser or a God-pleaser?"

One of the listeners that day was Phil. He sat there with his on-the-edge skater haircut and clothes, soaking it all in. Afterward, he said, "Yeah . . . I'm gonna get radical for God. Full-blown. Out there. In their face. Cool, c-ya."

The next day his teacher assigned him a paper called "My Life

Philosophy." Phil called me, "Yeah, it's due in two weeks. The teacher wants some of us to read our paper out loud to the class. I'm goin' for it. I want the whole class to know that Christ is my philosophy."

I wasn't sure if Phil would do it. At other times he had talked about "Sticking up for God and gettin' radical," but he didn't come through.

This time he did. Phil wrote a five-hundred-word paper telling how God had changed his life. He described how he used to like getting into trouble and basically showing off. Since he met Jesus, he was now living for God and not for himself.

The teacher was so impressed with his paper that she asked him to read it in front of the class.

Phil was very nervous as he read it. He knew that some people had no clue that he knew God. But as he read it, God gave him strength and boldness. People stared at him as he told them, "God is number one in my life."

At lunch that day, some of Phil's friends called him preacher, padre, and brother. They were putting him down for his statement about his faith. The next day, some of his friends avoided him, and he had to eat lunch alone. This went on for several days. It if weren't for his brother, Phil would have eaten lunch alone for weeks.

When we stand up for God, it can cost us. Friends. Popularity. Teasing. Weird looks.

Phil would tell you that it was worth it. Because he stood up for God that first time, it became easier. Before too long Phil's friends came back to him and asked why his faith meant so much to him. They asked how he could have peace inside when they were so angry and troubled. Phil was able to talk with them about his relationship with Jesus.

Phil learned that many opportunities come disguised as problems. He decided to take a risk for God.

Sometimes we become more concerned with our comfort than our convictions. We would rather be comfortable than right. But being a Christian means doing the right thing, even if it isn't easy.

> I have been crucified with Christ and I no longer live, but Christ lives in me. The life I live in the body, I live by faith in the Son of God, who loved me and gave himself for me (Gal. 2:20).

When Christ calls us, He calls us to come and die. That is why we wear crosses around our necks: we "have been crucified with Christ." God wants to make us into "little Christs." He wants us to become like His Son. But some of us are more concerned about comfort and acceptance than we are conviction and obedience. God is more committed to our character than our comfort. If following Jesus means comfort, then we would have little gold recliners on our necklaces instead of crosses. Following Jesus means going outside our comfort zones to do what He would do.

Which is it for you: convictions or comfort?

RESPONSE

1. What do you think of the saying "Opportunity comes disguised as a problem"?

2. If you were given the same assignment as Phil, what would you say is your life philosophy?

3. Why do you think some people tease you, or put you down, for standing up for your beliefs?

4. What would be some of the costs (in your life) if you were to make a radical stand for Christ?

5. What do you think about the concept that "God is more committed to our character than our comfort?"

A LETTER TO MY SON

Dear Son,

I know it's difficult to go to school some days. I know it's even more challenging if you are going to stand up for Christ. I wish that on those days you could clap your hands and a seven-foot bodyguard would appear—kind of like Shaquille O'Neal! That would be cool, but it's not likely to happen.

Remember you aren't alone. The strongest bodyguard on the planet goes to school with you every day. When you are being picked on for being a Christian, you can go to Him. He will give you protection and help you respond. That bodyguard, of course, is God. He is with you *all* the time. Notice that He doesn't whisk you out of the situation and pat you on the head saying, "Oh, you poor kid. I am sorry that you have to experience rejection!" God doesn't pull us *out* of trouble; He sees us *through* the trouble.

First Peter 2:19 reminds us to "praise the Lord if you are punished for doing right" (TLB). In fact, according to this verse, trouble might be part of His plan. There are certain lessons we can only learn if we are encountering opposition and tension. These challenges help refine us; they make us more like Christ.

I wish life would be easy and pain-free, but that is reserved for heaven. In the meantime, we know that we are going to encounter difficulties. Following Jesus means doing the right thing, even if it isn't easy.

Like going to the cross.

WWJD? What Would Jesus Do?

> Sacrificially yours,
> Dad

JOURNAL

Respond to the letter by writing your own thoughts here. Parents may want to use Tim's letter as a model for their own.

_____

_____

_____

_____

_____

_____

➡ CONNECTION ⬅

Rent the video *Ben Hur* and watch it together as teen and parent. Talk about the sacrifices people made to follow what they believed in.

An alternative video might be *Chariots of Fire*.

CHAPTER 27

SCHOOL: HOW DO YOU SPELL INTENSE?

School can be a weird place. Where else can you meet the girl of your dreams or Mrs. Raptor The Terrible as one of your teachers? It's definitely a mixed bag. But school is important. Where else could you learn useful stuff like the Pythagorean theorem or Norman's Invasion?

Here are some actual quotes taken from students' papers given to me by a friend who teaches high school somewhere in the continental United States. For obvious reasons, he wants to remain anonymous.

▶ "Without the Greeks we wouldn't have history. The Geeks invented three kinds of columns—Corinthian (named after the leather), Dorkic and Ironic."

▶ "Greeks also had lots of myths. A myth is a female moth."

▶ "It was the painter Donatello's interest in the female nude that made him the father of the Renaissance."

▶ "It was an age of great inventions and discoveries: Gutenberg invented the Bible. Sir Walter Raleigh invented cigarettes. Another important invention was the circulation of blood. And who could forget Sir Francis Drake who circumcised the world with a hundred-foot clipper?"

▶ "Bach was the most famous composter in the world and so was Handel. Handel was half German, half Italian, and half English. He was very large. Beethoven wrote music even though he was deaf. He was so deaf he wrote loud music. He took long walks in the forest, even when everyone was calling him. Beethoven expired in 1827, and later died for this."

School is the place where you learn critical facts like these.

In spite of all the humor and craziness, school is really important. It

influences your future. To maximize success in your future, let me
humbly introduce:

THE TEN COMMANDMENTS FOR STUDENTS

I. THOU SHALT GO TO SCHOOL

Someone once said, "Half of success in life is showing up." Make sure
you show up for class. Teachers like that kind of thing.

II. THOU SHALT BE PREPARED

Boy Scouts have been using this motto for years. Now it's time to use
it in the classroom. So bring your poncho, matches, and hatchet to class.
No, wait; be prepared with your books and all the materials you will need
in class. Thou shall not mooch off of thy neighbor.

III. THOU SHALT HONOR THY TEACHER

Honor means to show respect for the position and the person of the
teacher. The term comes from weighing gold and it literally means to
"make heavy." Something heavy is valuable. Consider your teacher, her
preparation, and her lesson plans as valuable. Honor her. If you honor a
person, you can learn from her.

IV. THOU SHALT BE ORGANIZED

Assignment notebooks are the greatest tools to help you remember
schoolwork. Write every assignment in one notebook and include all
instructions and due dates. Then, at the end of the day, read the assignment book and take home all the stuff you will need to work on that
night.

V. THOU SHALT NOT STEAL

I must admit, this one isn't original with me. God came up with it.
Cheating is stealing by benefiting from work you didn't do. I know some
people who work so hard at cheating that it would have been easier to
actually study! Cheating is dangerous because it is a deception and can
become addictive.

VI. THOU SHALT DO YOUR HOMEWORK

Most teenagers who struggle with school don't do their best when it
comes to their homework. They tend to blame others:

"I forgot my book and the school was locked."

"My dog ate my homework."

"I'm too busy feeding the homeless to get it done."

"Being in Javelin Catching takes all my time."

Schedule time every school night to get your homework done. Block out two hours. If you get done early, use the time to organize your notebook or read. You can read ahead in your text or in a book of your choice. But spend the full two hours doing work. Take a few breaks for a snack, but don't watch TV during homework time.

VII. THOU SHALT NOT FIGHT

All it takes is one fight to get out of hand, and you'll be dusted in your middle-school or high-school career. Even though you may feel like pounding a classmate, teammate, or teacher, don't. San Quentin prison has a lousy educational environment, but it does have a nice kiln for pottery projects.

VIII. THOU SHALT DRESS

Don't sweat it! I'm not talking about guys wearing dresses. I'm talking about suiting up for P.E. Gym clothes are carefully designed to be uncomfortable and to make you look like a geek. The coach with the funny, too-tight, polyester shorts has a clipboard and will take off points if you don't "suit-up." Grin and bear it. Everybody else looks as silly as you do. The more people suiting up, the more people to blend in with (or laugh at)!

IX. THOU SHALT HANG AROUND WITH LEARNERS

Try to hang with some students who are actually learning something at school; it might rub off. If you only hang with the spit-wad brigade or the Principal's Pals Posse, you may be in for some trouble. You don't have to do anything wrong at school to get in trouble; you only have to be *accused* of it.

X. THOU SHALT SEEK HELP

"The only stupid question is an . . . ? What class? That's right—the only stupid question is an *unasked* question. If you need help, simply ask for it. Put your pencil down. Stand on top of your desk and scream, "HELLLP!" Okay, I'm kidding about the screaming and the standing on your desk, but you can still ask someone for help. Try talking to your teacher, a counselor, or ask about tutors. You might be surprised by the number of students who have undercover tutors.

PROBLEM TEACHERS

You may be having trouble with a particular class, and you might think the teacher is out to get you. But it may not be the teacher as much as it is the subject. Is it a class you tolerate only because it is required? What time of day is the class? If it is first period, and you don't wake up until third period, this may account for some of the trouble. Any class at the end of the day automatically loses points because you are tired and have had it with school by then. My worst classes were right after lunch; I always wanted to take a siesta!

The harsh reality is that you may be stuck for the year. You can talk to the principal, but the reality is, you may have to learn to deal with a difficult teacher. How you respond in the situation is what will make the difference. You cannot change the teacher, but you can change your perspective. By now you might have an idea of why you are having the problem.

The next step is to take your eyes off the problem and put them on God.

When Peter walked to Jesus on the water, he did just fine until he took his eyes off the Lord and saw the enormous waves and choppy water. Then he began to sink. He cried out, "Lord, save me!" Immediately Jesus reached out His hand and pulled Peter to safety.

When you feel afraid, remember that the God of the universe is your guard. He will rescue you and protect you. He will keep you from being shamed. Believe it or not, you may learn lessons on life even at school!

RESPONSE

1. What do you think about the Ten Commandments for Students?
2. What are some traits of a terrible teacher?
3. Teens, ask your parents to describe their worst teachers.
4. What can you learn from a teacher you don't like?
5. How can keeping our eyes on God protect us?

A LETTER TO MY SON

Dear Son,

I wish I could guarantee a positive and stress-free learning environment for you at school. Schools aren't safe anymore. You can get shot just praying with your friends at the flagpole or studying with them in the library. Crazy, isn't it?

I wish I could keep you from embarrassment and hassle dished out by mean and hurtful teachers, but I can't.

I can't keep you from some of the pain in life. You will just have to experience it. Let's hope you can learn from it.

If you want, God can be your bodyguard. Ask Him to protect you from harmful words and experiences that may happen at school. Ask Him to rescue you from a teacher who may be abusive, or ask Him to give you the strength and endurance to hang in there.

God wants to be our refuge in life's storms—including those at school.

God can give you protection from people who will put you to shame. You know, the ones who make fun of you or put you down for what you believe? One way that God protects you is through me. If someone starts shaming you or picking on you, let me know. You don't have to be alone with it. Don't try to be the big, strong man who handles everything by himself. We will talk about it and figure out some course of action. Sometimes you challenge and sometimes you don't. Wisdom knows when to fight and when to walk away.

Learning with you,
Dad

"Hold on to instruction, do not let it go; guard it well, for it is your life" (Prov. 4:13).

JOURNAL

Respond to the letter by writing your own thoughts here. Parents may want to use Tim's letter as a model for their own.

_____

_____

_____

_____

_____

_____

_____

_____

➡ CONNECTION ⬅

School Days

Get out the parent's yearbook from high school and take a short trip down memory lane. Teens, ask your parent to show you his or her least favorite teacher and favorite teacher. Have fun looking at the fashions and haircuts. If you want, do the same thing with your yearbook.

CHAPTER 28

NO PAIN, NO GAIN

GOOD PAIN?
How could any pain be good?
I think I first heard the phrase "no pain, no gain" from my high school cross-country coach. Cross-country is one of those silly sports where you run up and down hills until you lose your lunch. You do this for six days so you can look good on meet day for the crowd that shows up: all six people. A spectator at a cross-country meet watches the beginning of the race and the end, usually missing the middle. That is probably why we only had six spectators.

It was at practice that coach said, "Come on, run through the pain. Make it hurt. It will pay off in the meet. *No pain, no gain.*"

Why did the mean coach say this?

Because he knew that running a lot was painful. Our bodies were screaming, *Why are you doing this to us? We will get back at you! Why didn't you go out for tennis or golf?* We were tempted to quit or slow down. Coach knew that it was important for us to endure the pain. It was part of conditioning. Sometimes the only difference between a good athlete and a premier athlete is his willingness to work through the pain. I have seen some athletes with less talent do better than gifted athletes because they were willing to work through the pain. *No pain, no gain.*

ERIC LIDDELL

When Eric Liddell ran, he tilted his head back and looked at the sky. When someone jokingly asked him how he knew where the finish line was, he replied, "The Lord guides me."

Eric was considered a contender for an Olympic gold in the 100-meter race in Paris. When he discovered that the trials were scheduled on a Sunday, he said, "I am not running. It is the Lord's Day." Even though he risked ridicule and pressure from others, he held his ground. As other racers qualified in the 100-meters, Eric was preaching in a Paris church. Later, he competed in the 200- and 400-meter races. Even though they weren't his best events, he did his best. He won a bronze medal in the 200 and a *gold* medal in the 400! In fact, he set a world record of 47.6 seconds! His story was told in the Oscar-winning movie *Chariots of Fire*.

Eric learned how to endure pain for the reward.

BAD PAIN

"How could kids be so cruel?"

"Where were their parents?"

"Why didn't somebody stop them?"

"Why did they kill people they knew?"

"Will I ever feel safe at school again?"

These were the questions that filled our heads for weeks after the shootings at Columbine High School in Littleton, Colorado.

It doesn't seem right, does it? It certainly doesn't seem fair. Why should two hate-filled students kill other students and a teacher and injure dozens of others? Some students face lifetime disabilities due to the noon-time barrage of the shooters.

Life isn't fair.

If God is so loving and powerful, why did He let this happen? In fact, why is there so much pain in the world?

Do you ever ask yourself these questions?

I do. Sometimes it seems like God takes the day off. In anger I demand, "Where were You? Why didn't You do something?"

Sometimes a loving God doesn't make sense. The world just seems too cruel for a "nice-guy God" to fit in.

The pain in the world is something we need to think about. We believe in a loving God, one who doesn't like suffering and is capable of stopping it. So why doesn't He?

God doesn't seem to be doing anything about violence, abuse, starving people, nuclear threat, cancer, and AIDS. Could God really stop all the pain and suffering in the world?

Yes, He could. And someday He will. But for right now we live in a world of free choice. Each of us has the choice to follow God and His way or to choose a different course.

According to Isaiah 53:6, we all have chosen our own selfish ways. God gave us real choices, and we have to live with the real consequences. God could have made us robotic clones that get up in the morning and say, "I love You, God. Plug in my software and I will do fully as I am programmed to do." But He didn't.

We were made with free moral choice. That means we have the freedom to decide whether or not we will follow God. It also means that we will have to face the consequences of our decisions (not to mention other people's decisions). Some of the major problems of this world are the outcome of sinful people making wrong choices.

Suffering and pain are not God's choice; they are a result of dozens and dozens of choices by sinful people. The good news is that Jesus has the power to overcome all suffering, even death. Jesus Himself went through incredible suffering and rejection. He died so our world could be delivered from the mess people created.

God is involved in our world and in our pain. He won't wave a magic wand and make pain disappear. But He can deliver us from the trap of sin and the despair of death. With Jesus, we share triumph over those very things that cause pain.

> "For I know the plans I have for you," declares the Lord,
> "plans to prosper you and not to harm you, plans to give you
> hope and a future. Then you will call upon me and come
> and pray to me, and I will listen to you" (Jer. 29:11-12).

It is God's desire to walk with us in our pain and to give us healing. In the midst of our recovery, He will give us hope and a future. This seems to be the way He works, whether we are suffering physical or emotional pain.

When things are comfortable, easy, and prosperous, I often ignore the gentle whisperings of my Heavenly Father. But in the agony and loneliness of pain, I hear His voice as if He's shouting.

> *"God seems to whisper to us in our prosperity but shout at*
> *us in our pain."*

RESPONSE

1. When does *no pain, no gain* apply to your life?
2. What kind of pain do you think surrounded the school shootings?
3. When do you feel life isn't fair?
4. Read Isaiah 53:6. What are the results of our choices?
5. How does God's promise for "hope and a future" help a person in pain?

A LETTER TO MY SON

Dear Son,

I wish I could protect you from pain and suffering. I wish I were that big and strong.

But I am not.

In fact, my protection might not even be good for you. Sometimes suffering produces what we need.

Luke was back in the hospital. It had become a familiar place in his short, twelve-year-old life. He was born with a respiratory disease that often forced him back to the hospital for treatment. He didn't like being confined indoors, but at least this time he had a window in his room. He spotted a butterfly cocoon on the window ledge. He kept a continual watch on the cocoon, because he knew a beautiful butterfly would one day emerge.

One day, he noticed the cocoon had come to life. *The butterfly is trying to get out!* Luke was excited to watch the butterfly battle to emerge from its dark, restrictive cocoon.

He watched for hours. The struggling insect seemed to have lost strength. It had stopped trying to emerge. Worried, Luke grabbed a pair of scissors and snipped the opening a little larger to help the butterfly. *I don't want her to struggle so much,* he thought.

The butterfly crawled out, but all it ever did was crawl! The stress of the struggle was necessary. The press of the wings against the cocoon forced colorful, life-giving juices back into the wings. But because Luke took a shortcut, the pretty butterfly that was designed to fly on rainbow wings was instead condemned to crawl in the dust.

Sometimes, son, the stress of struggle is necessary for our own good.

I know this goes against what we feel should be fair. *We should be able to lead fun, pain-free lives in the comfort of our homes.* But God isn't committed to our fun or comfort. His plan for prosperity and protection may or may not involve our physical lives. Consider the second part of Jeremiah 29:11-12: "Then you will call upon me and come and pray to me, and I will listen to you." God wants us to get close to Him when we are hurting. The emphasis isn't on the problem; it is on how close we are to God. God will allow problems into our lives if they are useful in pulling us closer to Him.

It is my prayer that the sufferings of life will draw you closer to God. I believe that is part of His plan to give you a hopeful future, one that keeps you close to Him.

As I said, I wish I could keep suffering away from you. But it helps to know that suffering has a purpose.

Hopefully yours,
Dad

Journal

Respond to the letter by writing your own here. Parents may want to use Tim's letter as a model for their own.

_____

_____

_____

_____

_____

_____

_____

_____

➤ CONNECTION ◀

Option 1: Take a field trip to a place where people are suffering: an emergency room, a funeral home, or a rescue mission. Discuss the questions below.

Option 2: Watch *ER* or *Chicago Hope* on TV. Discuss:

▶ What kinds of suffering did we see?

▶ What did they do to help with the suffering?

▶ How could God be with a person in the middle of that suffering?

▶ Is there anything we could do to help?

CHAPTER 29

WHEN FRIENDS DIE

can't believe he would do something like that. He knows better than to drink and drive!" Vince wiped the tears from his eyes. He reached for the tissues on my desk. He blew his nose and violently tossed the tissue into the trash. "Why Nick? Why did my friend have to die? He was only seventeen!"

Vince and Nick had known each other since third grade. They met that year because they were on the same soccer team, the Purple Panthers. They played together for years and became friends in middle school. Now they were on the high school soccer team. They had become best friends, closer than brothers. Homecoming was coming up and they were going to double date. They had great plans:

Homecoming.

Soccer season.

Surf all summer.

Their senior year.

They had lots of plans. Until the accident!

Nick went to a beach party and had a few beers. On the way home, he totaled his dad's truck. He was thrown from the cab and landed in a ravine. He wasn't wearing his seatbelt. His girlfriend, Tracy, was saved by the airbag. Nick was dead on arrival.

It did not seem right. It did not seem fair. *He was a young man, so full of promise. Now he was gone.*

All we can do is grieve.

Sometimes grief is like that. You need a time of sadness before you can go on with life.

Life is full of loses. If it's not losing dogs or grandmas, it's friends dying. Or for some, divorce is a sudden, intense loss. Grief can hit us in many ways, and each loss is different and unpredictable.

How do we handle grief? What are some ways to cope with loss? My personal experience may provide some answers.

TIM PINES

I can hardly put on a pair of beach sandals without thinking of Tim Pines. Tim always wore his thongs (rubber beach sandals), and in a way, they symbolized Tim: casual, comfortable, sensible, and affordable. No expensive leather dress shoes for this guy! Tim was always the first one to volunteer to do some lowly job on our youth ministry team. He didn't really care who got the credit, as long as we understood his service was his way to say thanks to God.

Tim always remembered that God loved him. God's love overwhelmed him.

I will never forget staring up at a desert sky filled with stars and hearing Tim say, "To think we are more significant to God than all of those."

Tim was a designer for Mazda. On a business flight to Tokyo, he jotted down some personal goals. "I will consider myself a success when I:

▶ am walking close with Christ every day.
▶ am living out *to live is Christ and to die is gain.*
▶ am building a strong and intimate marriage with my wife.
▶ am loving my kids with sacrificial love.
▶ am performing my job to the best of my abilities.
▶ am using all of my resources to point others to Christ."

Nature illustrated for Tim the awesome power of God. It is ironic that he should die in a freak avalanche in Southern California, just two weeks after he wrote these goals!

I miss Tim. I wish he were still here; we could go surfing. Then we could talk about the power of God as seen in the ocean.

I know he is in heaven. We will catch up when I get there.

Do you ever wonder, *What will it be like in heaven?*

Heaven is going to be good. When a Christian dies, his body quits working, but his soul is "at home with the Lord" (2 Cor. 5:8). Heaven is our eternal home. That's why when someone dies, we sometimes call it a "home-going."

> Do not let your hearts be troubled. Trust in God; trust also in my Father's house are many rooms. . . . I am going there to prepare a place for you. . . . I will come back and take you to be with me (John 14:1-3).

If Jesus is making our home, it is really going to be something! Look at the world He created in six days! Can you imagine what heaven will be like if He is preparing a place for us for over two thousand years?

There will be no fear when we die, because the essence of us, our real nature, will be with Jesus. Another thing that will happen at the time the Bible calls "the last trumpet" is that all Christians will be given new spiritual bodies. (See 1 Corinthians 15.) Whenever the last trumpet call occurs, all believers will be changed in a "flash, in the twinkling of an eye."

That is bound to be an incredible sight; imagine how awestruck we will be. I will also feel relieved to no longer have my old body, won't you? No more groaning in front of the mirror and trying to make the best of what I've got. We will have new bodies. Just think—you will look fine every day!

Death is powerful and permanent, but God is even stronger.

> He will swallow up death forever. The Sovereign Lord will wipe away the tears from all faces; he will remove the disgrace of his people from all the earth. The Lord has spoken (Isa. 25:8).

We have so many losses on this planet. Death is a tragic loss. It will be awesome to see God "swallow up death." He is powerful, but he is also caring and personal. *He will wipe away the tears from our faces.*

God loves us so much that He helps us face the thing we fear the most: death. He promises eternal life, in which we won't be trapped and weighed down with the disgrace of sin. We will be set free to enjoy eternity with the *one who knows us best and loves us most.*

OSCAR DIEGO

My friend Oscar died. He was a faithful, dearly loved junior high pastor. It was on one of the junior high events that Oscar drowned in the lake. He left behind a young wife, an infant son, and a stunned youth group.

I struggled with God's choice. *Why Oscar? Why not someone else? Why now?*

I really didn't receive answers when I asked these questions, but I received God's comfort. I was reminded of the thousands of lives Oscar touched in twenty-nine short years. I am comforted knowing Oscar is in heaven now. He is probably playing basketball on the celestial courts!

Heaven is incredibly beautiful. There is no darkness or night. God is the source of heaven's light. In heaven we won't be worried or angry, because God will be our peace. We will no longer feel sad, because God will wipe away every tear. We will be perfectly happy because we will be living exactly according to our designer's plan.

When I think about where Tim and Oscar are and what they are experiencing, it helps me work through my grief. I imagine that Oscar has met Tim by now, and they are probably doing every extreme sport in heaven!

Do you suppose there's snowboarding in heaven?

RESPONSE

1. What would you say to Vince if he were your friend?
2. What has been your closest experience with the death of a person?
3. What do you think of the phrase that describes God as *one who knows us best, and loves us most?*
4. What do you think about the stories of Tim and Oscar?
5. What do you think heaven will be like?

A LETTER TO MY SON

Dear Son,

Death is a painful topic. It's not one that is popular at dinner parties, but it is just as real as anything else. Some would argue that death is not something to talk about with your teenager, but I disagree. If we can talk about death, we can talk about life. The purpose of these discussions is to talk about important issues.

What could be more important than death? It is the ultimate issue. For a believer, death isn't final. It is more of a stage you go through. Death stands

as a page between the two chapters of physical life and eternal life.
When someone dies, I find great comfort in God's promise:

> "Death has been swallowed up in victory."
>> "Where, O death is your victory?
>> Where, O death, is your sting?"
> The sting of death is sin, and the power of sin is the law. But thanks be to God! He gives us the victory through our Lord Jesus Christ (1 Cor. 15:54-57).

Christians don't have to be defeated by death. If we have a friend who dies, who is a believer, we will grieve the loss, but we won't grieve as though we don't have hope. We have hope in the Resurrection. Just as Christ defeated death, so will our friend conquer death because of his faith in the risen Christ.

Death doesn't defeat a Christian.

We don't have to be afraid of death. We know that the Resurrection waits for us on the other side. There are many people who are stressed about their lives and health and who worry about their death. They are trying to capture eternity in their hands. When it evades them, they become discouraged.

Christ has already dealt with death: He gave it a death sentence. He promises eternal life to all who believe. For me, this is greatly encouraging and helps reduce my anxiety about life.

It means that Christ wants to stay connected with us forever. Death does not separate us from God's love. Death is the mightiest foe we face as humans, but God's love is greater still.

Wow! I feel really loved!

Living in love,
Dad

Journal

Respond to the letter by writing your own thoughts here. Parents may want to use Tim's letter as a model for their own.

_____

_____

_____

_____

_____

_____

_____

_____

_____

➡ CONNECTION ⬅

Visit a cemetery. Spend time reading the gravestones. Try to find the one with the most unusual slogans or circumstances. Bring along a Bible and read 1 Corinthians 15:35-57.

After a few minutes of discussion, be quiet and reflect on your feelings.

"Christianity is a great way to live and the only way to die."

CHAPTER 30

SHOW ME THE MONEY!

Y ou may not be one of the characters on *Beverly Hills 90210,* so you probably have limited funds. Instead of driving a Porsche, you may be stuck with a Sprint. Or the bus. Your jewelry probably didn't come from Rodeo Drive. You bought it on sale at Wal-Mart. It doesn't matter where you live, or how much money your folks have, every teen needs cash.

Let's take a look at a typical month: Athletic shoes could set you back $100. To stay alive, you gotta have your fast food: eight #1 combos supersized cost $40. You must have a social life, so one movie a week could cost you $32. A quick cruise of the mall can set you back $50 or more for just *one* clothing item! That must-have new CD will lighten your wallet by $16. This adds up to $238 in one month, and you haven't even gone out on one date, let alone a prom or to some big dance or amusement park. It's just your basic month.

As a teenager you are a consumer: you need shoes, food, entertainment, and clothes to survive. Many companies are interested in you. They study and watch teens. They try to catch your attention. They don't do this just to be cool; they want to sell you something. Your generation represents millions of teenagers and billions of dollars.

Where are you going to get $238 a month? Allowance? For some, your parents will cover you, but for many, you will need to get a job. Some can work around the house to pick up extra cash, but that may not be enough.

With all of the usual pressure to have the right things and fit in, you may be forced to get a job. Most parents draw the line on what they will buy you. Some teens decide to get their stuff the old fashioned way: *they earn it.* Jobs for teenagers can vary as much as teen haircuts—some are great and some are hideous. Knowing what to look for and avoid will help.

The following list tells what to avoid in teen jobs:

BAD TEEN JOBS

1. The *graveyard shift:* midnight to eight A.M.
2. The *graveyard shift* at a graveyard.
3. Fast food job that pays you in french fries.
4. Jobs that make you *assistant manager* your first week.
5. Jobs that leave no time for homework.
6. Jobs that leave no time for friends, activities, or youth group.
7. Jobs with bosses who think you have no other life.
8. Cleaning up radioactive waste at the nuclear power plant (a job I had as a teenager).
9. Feeding the sharks at Sea World.
10. Sleep research subject.

What should you look for in a teen job? *One that pays you outrageously and requires that you do very little actual work.*

Realistically, consider:

WHAT TO LOOK FOR IN A JOB

1. A boss who understands teens and their world.
2. A place that has other teens working there or else people you can relate to.
3. A schedule offering flexibility.
4. Clearly defined expectations, such as a written job description.
5. A position that challenges you to develop useful skills.
6. A boss who realizes that school comes first.
7. A workplace that pays on time and fairly.
8. A company with a good reputation in the community and among other workers.
9. A job that's safe and doesn't threaten your health, body, or sleep and that you are proud to work at and can talk about.
10. Employees who would be a good influence on you.

WHAT ABOUT THE MONEY?

Now that you have your dream job, what do you do with the money? "Spend it!"

Before you blow it on video games, Jujubes, and movies, consider a plan to help your money grow. The secret to making your money grow is not spending it all. You have to invest some. Let's say you go to work at Greasy Burger and you make $7 per hour, and you usually work ten hours a week. You gross $70, but Uncle Sam whittles it down to $55. What should you do with your fifty-five bucks?

Here are some tips:

1. Invest in things that increase in value.

Most of what you buy decreases in value the second you buy it. CDs, clothes, video games, and sporting goods are some examples. Things that go up in value (usually) are: gold, coins, money market accounts, certificates of deposit, mutual funds, stocks, and bonds.

2. Don't borrow money; avoid credit.

Credit can be a trap, especially when you are young. Pay cash and you will have the financial freedom you need.

3. If you must borrow money, don't use it for things that decrease in value.

Sometimes the pressure to get something forces us to buy it on credit. These are dangerous impulse buys. Most things we buy like this will not be worth what you have to pay for them once you figure in all of the finance charges. Borrowing money makes sense if you are buying something that increases in value. Some houses and a few cars are examples.

I bought a Mustang, drove it for ten years, and sold it for more than I paid for it!

4. Invest in things that stay ahead of inflation.

You may have more *discretionary* income than your parents. That is the money you get to choose how to spend. Your parents are stuck with big and boring bills like the house payment, utilities, insurance, and your braces. How should you spend your hard-earned cash?

Let's say you have $55 a week or about $238 a month.

1. Give a portion of your first cash to God: your church, your youth group, missions etc. Ten percent is a good place to start ($5.50 per week).

2. Open an interest-bearing savings account with $25. (Some banks offer free checking to students in combination with a savings account and ATM card.)
3. Forget you have it. Let it collect interest.
4. Once a month, put in $25.
5. Make a budget for the rest. Decide in advance how you will spend it. Write it down. Keep a record. You might want to use *Quicken* or some other software.

   Example: Monthly Budget Income $238.00
Giving	$23.00
Savings	$25.00
Living	$190.00

   How it might be spent:
$50.00	Food
$50.00	Entertainment
$50.00	Clothes/gifts

   That still leaves $40 for other things.

6. Consider increasing your savings with some of this extra cash. When you reach $500 in savings, purchase a certificate of deposit. It's called a CD. It will earn you more interest. They come in three-month, six-month, or one-year terms.
7. Option: Start studying mutual fund investments by reading money magazines or on-line information. Become familiar with the funds you like and that perform well. You might also do the same for stocks. Before you invest, you will need your parent's approval and $500 to $1000 minimum investment. Don't invest it all in one place; this makes your money more secure.
8. Start thinking about long-term savings for a car, college, golf clubs for Dad, etc.
   5. *Invest on a regular basis (weekly or monthly).*

Discipline yourself to stick to your budget. If you have the impulse to blow your budget and buy something, apply the *Forty-eight-Hour Rule.* Wait two days and see if it still is worth it. Chances are, you will cool your heels and be able to stick to your budget. A budget is *your plan to get what you want*. You do yourself a favor when you stick to it.

6. Invest in things that last.

If you are a Christian, you will want to invest in building God's kingdom. That is why you want to give the first portion of your income to God and His work on earth: church, missions, youth ministries, etc. When you give as worship and gratefulness to God, you are investing in His kingdom and are helping others know and experience His love.

I know some parents may be surprised that I have spent a whole chapter on money. But according to a recent Gallup Survey, the number one topic that teens wish they had more information on and discussion with their parents was money.

Jesus spent much of His teaching time on the topic of money. If Jesus talked about it, and our teens want to talk about it, it makes sense that we discuss it with them.

RESPONSE

1. How does TV portray teens and money?
2. Is $238 a month realistic for you? What would you change?
3. In your opinion, what would be a bad teen job? What would be your ideal teen job?
4. What did you think about the six tips on money and the sample budget?
5. Why give to God? *(Does He really need my $5?)*

A LETTER TO MY SON

Dear Son,

I was speaking at a high school winter camp, and I felt led to speak on money. Usually, I go for the sure-bet talks like sex, dating, and friends. But I was sensing that a lot of teens and their parents were stressed about finances.

I read from the Bible:

Command those who are rich in this present world not to be

> arrogant nor to put their hope in wealth, which is so uncer-
> tain, but to put their hope in God, who richly provides us with
> everything for our enjoyment. Command them to do good, to
> be rich in good deeds, and to be generous and willing to
> share (1 Tim. 6:17-18).

I explained, "Confidence shouldn't be in our wealth. We can easily lose it all on any given day. Our hope needs to be in God. Our investments should follow our hearts. If our hope is in God, then some of our money should be used to advance His kingdom. God wants us to enjoy the things He has given us, but He also wants us to be good managers of our wealth and resources by generously sharing with others."

After my talk, a very troubled sixteen-year-old girl came up to me and asked, "Is it wrong to be wealthy?" She dabbed at her tears.

"No, it's not wrong. Money isn't the root of all evil, it's the *love* of money that causes grief." (See 1 Timothy 6:10.)

She looked a little relieved. "Oh, that's good, because we are very wealthy. We help lots of people and give to the church and missions. I just didn't know if you were saying it's wrong."

"No—greed is wrong. Being rich isn't. In fact, wealth can give you free-dom and choices that poverty doesn't. If you have money, you can choose to help people. I believe God expects rich people to be responsible with their wealth. Jesus said that if we were given much, much would be expected of us."

She blew her nose and wiped smeared mascara from her eyes. "Well, that makes me feel so much better. I want to be able to use my money to help other people. Today, I made a decision to use all that I have and am to help others know Christ."

"A wise decision."

She walked away smiling. She truly is the wisest of investors.

Son, I hope you can be like this girl. I don't even know her name; she never told me. Let's just call her Wise Woman.

Invest in the best,

Dad

JOURNAL

Respond to the letter by writing your own thoughts in the section below. Parents may want to use Tim's letter as a model for their own.

_____

_____

_____

_____

_____

_____

_____

_____

➤ CONNECTION ◀

Take ten one-dollar bills and put them on the table. Get paper, pen, and a Bible each for teen and parent. Set a timer for ten minutes. See who can find and write the most verses from the Bible that talk about money, wealth, mammon, etc. To count, you must write the entire verse and the reference.

After ten minutes (when the buzzer goes off), stop and count. Read each of the verses. Give a dollar for each verse and reference. If you each have the verse, place that dollar in the middle of the table. Add up your money and decide how you want to spend it. Ideas may include:

1. Go out for ice cream. The one with the most money gets a banana split; the "loser" gets a single-scoop cone.

2. Give the "in-the-middle-money" to a family member. Go out for your favorite fast food, spending only what you earned. Have the family member join you.

CHAPTER 31

RECRUITING A COACHING TEAM

arry Walters lives in the suburbs just south of the Los Angeles Airport (LAX). Larry is a truck driver who likes to spend his weekends relaxing in his backyard in his reclining lawn chair. One day, he got a bright idea: *I will buy weather balloons, fill them with helium and tie them to my lawn chair. I will take my BB gun and shoot out a balloon if I get too high. Won't my neighbors think this is cool!*

He did it. He actually went through with it! Larry got thirty weather balloons, filled them with helium and tied them to his lawn chair. With snacks and his BB gun in hand, he had his friends release him. He expected to rise to one hundred feet, but he shot straight up to eleven thousand feet! *This was not part of the plan!*

Larry didn't want to shoot out the balloons, because he was afraid it would cause his chair to get off balance and he would fall out. He floated into the landing pattern for LAX.

A Continental pilot of a DC-10 reported to air traffic control that he saw a lawn chair floating by. I wonder if he said to the passengers on the intercom, "We have begun our final descent to Los Angeles. If you look out on your right, you will see Hollywood. If you look out the left side of the plane, you will see a man in a lawn chair having a snack. Thank you for flying Continental."

Larry hung on for dear life. Helicopters were sent up to observe and escort him. LAX was shut down for hours. Eventually, the helium leaked out and Larry descended to earth. Television crews and huge crowds met up with him.

"Were you scared?" asked a TV reporter.

"What kind of question is that?" responded Larry. "Wouldn't *you* be scared if you were floating around in a lawn chair at eleven thousand feet?"

Another reporter cut in. "Are you going to do it again?"

"NO!"

"What in the world made you do it in the first time?" asked a third.

"Well, you can't just sit there!" explained Larry.[1]

The moral of this true story is: *When you allow your own thinking rather than God's wisdom to guide you, you will most likely end up off course.*

Larry trusted in his own thinking. It made sense to him to tie balloons to his lightweight chair and see if it would fly. It never occurred to him that he might fly too high or into the approach of dozens of jumbo jets.

What seems right to a person is not always right. Proverbs 1:7 reminds us that "The fear of the Lord is the beginning of knowledge, but fools despise wisdom and discipline." When we make God number one or Lord of our lives, and fear (show reverence to) Him, that leads to knowledge. But if we act as though we know it all, that leads to foolishness.

Fools trust in their own resources. Wise people trust in God and are open to learn. Fools act like know-it-alls.

Wisdom has been defined as *seeing life from God's perspective.* This means taking a look at life from a spiritual as well as physical perspective. It means taking the long-term view instead of the short-term view. It means being willing to look at things so differently that you might stand apart from the crowd.

Wisdom is acquired. It doesn't come naturally. It doesn't come easily. Much of what comes easily in life is just the opposite of wisdom.

Wisdom can't be given; it must be earned. Wisdom is forged on the anvil of life's experience. In other words, you can't shortcut the process of getting wisdom. In fact, most wisdom is gained through adversity.

Wisdom is not obtained in isolation. It is born out of community. We gain wisdom by talking, copying, listening, and relating to others. We are *taught* to seek wisdom: "Wisdom is supreme; therefore get wisdom" (Prov. 4:7).

How do you get wisdom?

By asking others to mentor you.

A mentor is someone who guides and connects with someone who has less experience. To gain wisdom, we need *wisdom mentors*, people who will help us develop wisdom.

SELECTING A WISDOM COUNCIL

Select three to seven mentors who will build a relationship with you and seek to help you develop qualities or skills. The mentors should meet with you at least once to share from their personal experience. Say that one of the qualities you want to develop is compassion; consider someone who must have compassion to do his daily work; a social worker, nurse, doctor, or counselor. When looking for someone to serve as mentor, consider the following characteristics.

QUALITIES OF A MENTOR

1. Integrity: Evidences the quality or skill you seek to gain.
2. Flexible: Adaptable and understands young people.
3. Available: Has time to share.
4. Relational: Is willing to connect with you.
5. Trainer: Able to empower you with the desired resource.

There are many ways to structure time with your mentor. One common way is to have six mentors work with you on six key relationships:

1. A man and his God
2. A man and his family
3. A man and his friends
4. A man and his job or school
5. A man and his girlfriend or spouse
6. A man and his world

These six mentors could include a grandparent or older relative who has influenced the young man's life. The other five mentors could be a pastor or youth worker, a teacher or coworker, a parent, coach, or friend. The mentors who make up the Wisdom Council seek to develop wisdom in a particular area of the young man's life.

Their responsibilities include:

1. Meet at least one time with you (preferably two or three times).
2. Assign projects that will develop the desired skill.

3. Develop a short three- to five-minute talk.

4. Present the talk publicly at a rite-of-passage event.

5. Give a copy of the talk notes to you.

6. Participate in some meaningful gift to memorialize the event.

THEMES TO CONSIDER

Besides the six key relationships as a theme for the mentoring process, consider the following, or make up your own:

Three Cords—Based on Ecclesiastes 4:12, "a cord of three strands is not quickly broken," develop three key qualities: spiritual, emotional, and social cords. For more information on this see *Family Traditions* (J.Otis Ledbetter and Tim Smith; pages 16-17).

Character Qualities—Choose ones such as compassion, integrity, dependability, etc., and support with Scripture and biblical examples of people who modeled these traits.

Meaning of Your Name—Research what your name means and its implications and applications for today. Some Christian bookstores have books and art built around this concept.

Bible Character—Design a mentoring approach focused on a man in the Bible. Deal with the themes of "How did God use him?" "How did God prepare him?" "What unique qualities does he have?"

Family Creed—Reinforce your family's creed by selecting aspects that you want to incorporate into your life. For more information on how to develop a family creed, see *Family Traditions* (pages 113-117).

A MILESTONE LETTER

My friend Robin Spurlock has had a long and effective ministry in camping and youth ministry. She tells how her family provided a significant rite of passage in her life as a teenager:

"For my sixteenth and eighteenth birthdays, my family and significant others wrote letters affirming the growth they had seen in my life. They noted the growth of my character and evidence of spiritual growth. They reflected on the past and anticipated a favorable future."

These are the kinds of memories parents want to be building in the lives of young men. We want them launching into adulthood with confidence and the support of wise mentors. We want them making wise choices that will favor them with a positive future.

RESPONSE

1. What did you think of Larry's Lawn Chair Adventure?

2. How does trusting in our own thinking lead us to be off course?

3. What do you think about the statement *wisdom can't be given; it must be earned*?

4. What qualities would you like in a mentor?

5. Review the different themes for mentoring on page 187. Which mentoring theme appeals to you?

A LETTER TO MY SON

Dear Son,

I want to be a mentor to you, coaching you in wisdom and in life skills. That is why I am writing these letters. I want to make a difference; I want you to know that I care. I don't want to passively sit back and do nothing. I don't want to say in five years, "I wish I had done it differently. I wish I was more involved with my son."

I will be working on being a parent with *integrity*. I want my actions to match my words. I hope that you learn this trait by watching me.

I also want to be *flexible*. You don't have to be perfect. (Hey, you don't even have to be like me!) You can be yourself, and I will accept you for who you are—uniquely made in God's image—different, distinct, and valuable.

I want to be *available* to you. I will try to keep our regular times together going. They mean a lot to me. If we can keep meeting, it will help us develop a strong connection. That is my desire, to have an empowering *relationship* with you.

I hope to be a *trainer* for you, someone who helps you learn the skills and fundamentals that lead to effective living.

I want to be all these things to you, but I can't do it alone. That is why I will be working with you to develop our Wisdom Council—people who will love

and guide you as mentors. With their help, you will become a wise young
man prepared to take on life with confidence. You will be a "man with skills."

Seeking wisdom with you,
Dad

JOURNAL

Respond to the letter by writing your own thoughts here. Parents may
want to use Tim's letter as a model for their own.

_____

_____

_____

_____

_____

_____

_____

_____

_____

➡ CONNECTION ⬅

Separately, as parent and teen, complete the following. Then compare what you have written. Next, try to develop a plan that will address
the skills as mentoring areas.

Skills a Young Man Needs:

To make wise decisions:
Physical issues, such as _____
Social issues, such as _____
Spiritual issues, such as _____
Mental issues, such as _____

To possess character:
Qualities needed most include_____

To have vision and purpose:
My vision (clear mental picture of what I want to do) is _____
_____

My purpose (why I am here) is _____
_____

To have and use critical life skills:
At home (circle your selections): cook, drive, sew, iron, care for clothes, house cleaning and maintenance, yard work, shopping, planning a menu, and home organization.

Personal skills (circle your selections): budgeting, managing a checkbook, giving, using credit, saving, exercise and health tips, personal organization, and time management.

Interpersonal skills (circle your selections): reconciliation, setting boundaries, poise, manners, and conversation.

Review the skills again. This time ask, "Who could serve as a mentor for these different skills?" Write their names in the margin. If you want, contact each person and see if he would be willing to mentor you in their area of strength.

---

1 Jim Burns and Greg McKinnon, *Illustrations, Stories, and Quotes to Hang Your Message On* (Ventura, CA: Gospel Light Publications, 1997) 97.

CHAPTER 32

MONUMENTS

The mass of humans on the desert floor looked like lizards scurrying around. I observed them from my perch in the helicopter, two thousand feet above. They seemed to move about as they wished. They would walk in one direction for a few paces, stop and talk with someone, then walk in another direction. As we descended to one thousand feet, I noticed that the humans restricted their movements to a half-mile square. They didn't go beyond this block. Some went to the edges and loitered there. Others chose to linger around the middle where most of the humans congregated.

There were thousands of humans in this dry patch of sand. I didn't understand why they did not go beyond the borders of the box they had restricted themselves to. There were no fences, guards, or signs—just scrub oak, manzanita, and cacti.

As we prepared to land on the edge of the imaginary border, I noticed that all of these humans were teenage boys, some thirteen, some sixteen; others looked to be nineteen or twenty-something. They were from different races, wearing a variety of hairstyles and clothing, but they had something in common. Each boy walked quickly but aimlessly about, confusion stamped on his face.

Lost boys. They looked as if they were free, choosing to walk in one direction, stopping to chat quickly with another, then veering off on a new course. But as I observed their patterns, it was clear that they had very little freedom and no real direction. They were aimless. They had no meaningful conversations. They were not connected. They were active but made no progress. In a word, they were lost.

What appears as freedom and activity from a distance above is actually captivity and confusion up close. We have misread these boys, thinking they would prefer to be left alone. Abandoned boys desperately need guides who will direct them out of the confines of their desert existence. They need guides who know the path of being a teenage boy.

The helicopter stirred up an avalanche of dust. Some of the boys noticed and headed toward us; others noticed, but indifferently returned to their pacing. Still others didn't even notice; they were too involved in their search for signs and guideposts. As some of them approached the helicopter, they picked up rocks. They didn't know if we had come as friends or enemies.

"We come in peace!" I shouted over the churning blades. The engine was off, but the whir of the blades was noisy and stirred up gravel and dust.

The boys shielded their eyes with their hands. They squinted toward me. The blistering desert sun backlit the chopper and me.

"We mean no harm. We have come to ask you one question."

The bigger ones, at the front of the herd, fingered their rocks. Their cautious eyes ran over me, from toe to head. They weren't sure what to think. They weren't used to having someone come to their land. They weren't used to having someone talk with them. And they certainly weren't used to having someone ask for their opinion.

We are boys, what do we know?

A large boy, about six-foot-five, stepped out from the pack. His arms were muscular and his chest was huge. He had the powerful body of a warrior. But there was something about his face; it looked innocent and mystified. He had the face of a boy and the body of a man. He spoke. "What is your one question? Be quick, we have things to do."

"I will be brief," I promised. "My one question is 'When does a boy become a man?'"

The man/boy shook his head. "What did you say?" He put the rock down in his left hand. He held another in his right. With his left hand, he scratched his head. He cast a puzzled look toward the others.

They returned his look.

"Repeat the question," he demanded.

"When does a boy become a man?" I repeated with increased volume. Silence.

A tentative voice broke from the back, "I have an idea . . . um . . . a boy becomes a man when he is good at sports?"

"Thank you. Who else?"

"A boy becomes a man when he has sex with a girl?"

"No, that's not what I am looking for."

"Well, what are you looking for?" demanded the man/boy impatiently. "What do we get if we guess it—money? What is this, *Who Wants to Be a Millionaire?*" He glanced around and gathered the others' full attention. With sarcasm dripping he mocked, *"Is that your final answer?"*

The boys laughed.

"You will win the right to be a man, with all of its privileges and responsibilities."

Their eyes were riveted on me. I had spoken about the *lost sign.* I had struck a nerve. Collectively and individually they were on the quest to manhood. *How does one begin the journey to manhood?*

"When does a boy become a man?" I asked.

"Through achievement. If you get good grades and produce, then you are a man."

"What else?"

"What about this one?" asked a boy of about fifteen who stood on the fringe of the group, "A boy becomes a man when he gets all the stuff he wants."

I shook my head. "No."

"When I get my driver's license?"

"When I start smoking?"

"When I can drink beer?"

"When I can join the army?"

"No, no, NO!"

"We don't know when a boy becomes a man!" exclaimed the man/boy, "Stop taunting us. We don't even know *how* a boy becomes a man!" He threw his rock at my feet and stomped off.

The others followed; they immediately went back to what they were doing before: walking aimlessly, looking around pointlessly, and mumbling to themselves. But now they had picked up the pace.

RESPONSE

1. What do you think about the lost boys story?

2. Why were these boys walking without direction? Why were they able to only have short, but meaningless conversations with each other?

3. The lost boys picked up rocks. What does that reveal about teenage boys?

4. "When does a boy become a man?" was the question. Do their answers reflect what boys would say?

5. What is the "lost sign"? What do boys need to guide them?

A LETTER TO MY SON

Dear Son,

It can be frightening to be alone in the desert. It's not much more comforting to be with others yet still be lost. The desert is not a bad place if you are prepared for it. But we have been sending our boys to the desert of adolescence unprepared. We have assigned boys in our culture to an emotional relocation camp.

In other cultures, boys have rites of passage that prepare them for manhood. These are like road signs along the way directing and affirming a young man's progress. We miss these monuments in our culture. We don't have a way to train you for being a man. We need an *initiation* to manhood.

Probably, one of the best examples I can think of is the Jewish Bar Mitzvah. The Jewish people have understood the need to invest in raising sons who are prepared for manhood. You have some friends who have celebrated their Bar Mitzvah, and I am glad you were able to attend one.

As you know, the boy is taught to read the Bible by his father or another man. He studies it for a year or more and is tested to see if he really understands the concepts and the history of his people. At the public ceremony he must recite and sing from the Torah.

He is affirmed as a "son of the covenant" and accepted as "manhood material." He knows exactly what he needs to do to fully become a man: marry a devout Jewish woman, become a father, master a trade or career, and serve his community and synagogue.

It's clear. The quest to become a man is defined. *Just follow the steps.*

For most non-Jewish boys, the path isn't so clear. The boy may grow up with a mother who wants him to be different from what his father wants. His mother and father are possibly divorced. The boy receives a mixed message: *Should I be more like what my mom wants and less like what my dad wants?*

As a result of the confusion, he will ignore them both. *They don't care anyway. They seem too busy. Besides, I can turn to my friends for what I need.*

Son, this is what is happening to millions of boys in our culture. Cast off by those who claim to love them, they seek connection with and direction from peers. They pretend to be men long before they are.

Boys maturing badly.

I want you to know, son, that your mom and I are together on this; we want you to grow up to be a mature man of God. We have some specific goals in mind and will talk more about that later. We will take time to develop rites of passage and celebrate them with you. Your teenage years are a time for you to become an individual, but they are also a time for you to connect with men who can help point the way. Every boy needs a support team to help him navigate his teen years. Without support and guidance through his teen years, a boy is destined to become a *lost boy.*

> Your guide,
> Dad

JOURNAL

Respond to the letter by writing your own thoughts in the section below. Parents may want to use Tim's letter as a model for their own.

_____

_____

_____

_____

_____

_____

_____

_____

_____

◆ CONNECTION ◆

Faith Timeline

With construction paper or poster board, make a timeline of your faith journey. Illustrate any of the key events with drawings, clippings, computer art, photos, etc. Start with birth and leave some space for the years ahead to update it. When it is completed, get together with your parent (or teen) to discuss.

Some events might include: pre-birth dedication, birth, infant dedication, becoming a member of God's family, baptism, confirmation, rite-of-passage ceremony, high school graduation, engagement, marriage.

For the events that are in the future, record some ideas for developing monuments and rites of passage on your faith timeline.

CHAPTER 33

RITES OF PASSAGE

W hy do kids join gangs? Is it for the thrill?" The radio interviewer directed his question to me.

I was a little nervous; this was a live, national interview. I didn't want to mess up. "I believe some teens join gangs because they have a need to connect. They need to belong. Adults should mentor and nurture our teenage boys to provide them with steps to manhood, steps that we celebrate and affirm with rites of passage."

"There are rites of passage for a gang. Getting beat up by the gang is one initiation I am aware of," said the host. "Are there others?"

"Yes, most gangs now have stepped up the initiation. Many require you to do a drive-by to become a full-fledged member."

"A drive-by shooting, just so you can belong?"

"Teen boys have a strong desire to connect. We have misread them. We think they are on the road to becoming individuals, so we leave them alone. We abandon boys when they need us the most."

"But they don't act like they need us."

"It is an *act*. When a teen is pushing you away, his fingers are hoping to keep you close. The "get away!" means "give me space, but don't leave me." Teen boys need attention, structure, discipline, nurturing, moral direction, accountability, and spiritual growth in a community that cares about them. In a word, teens need mentors."

"That's intriguing. We have done just the opposite. We have a *boys will be boys* mindset and leave them to their own foolishness with our *hands-off* approach. We are now bearing the fruit of teenagers being on their own for twenty years or so. The school shootings could be an indicator of their lack of direction. Would you agree?"

"Absolutely. Boys' need for direction is hardwired into them. The teen years are the time when a boy learns and activates the ideals of manhood, ideals he will seek to follow the rest of his life. The boy who learns and embraces the manhood ideals becomes a man. A boy who does not wastes his teen years; he is at-risk and likely to create problems for himself and others. Violence, like the school shootings, is just one example of unguided boys who don't know how to become men."

"To a school shooter, being a man might mean *having power and dominating people*. It gets further twisted when he has his hands on automatic weapons."

"We need positive rites of passage. We need to affirm our boys and show them the way."

THE VOID

Our culture doesn't offer many rites of passage. The big ones include getting a driver's license and graduating from high school. Becoming an adult at eighteen doesn't provide much excitement. It actually becomes more of a burden. As a result, we have not taken the time to memorialize the growth of a young man. We have missed out on opportunities to affirm the masculinity of young men.

Ceremonies are those special events that make life memorable. Birthdays. School awards assemblies. Athletic banquets. Baptism. Graduations. Weddings. We remember because of ceremony.

Chances are, the more memorable events of your life surrounded a ceremony. Ceremonies don't just happen. Someone has to seize the opportunity to plan the event, invite people, decorate, arrange for food, design the program, and buy the gifts or awards. All of this work is intended to make you feel special. That's why the event is memorable.

Ceremonies are key events that are designed to honor a person at a memorable time in his life. As mentioned in the previous chapter, Jewish families provide a significant rite of passage with their son's Bar Mitzvah. Why would Jewish families invest so much in one celebration that lasts a few hours?

Because it is a key event designed to honor their son at a memorable time in his life.

In our Christian tradition we lack this rite of passage. We need some form of "initiation" ceremony that welcomes boys into manhood, causing the event to live on in a teenager's memory. The following is a description of a ceremony a parent could plan.

SEVEN KEYS TO A MEMORABLE CEREMONY

First, *make your ceremony experiential.* It isn't just an event; it is an experience. Ask yourself, "What do I want people to experience when they receive the invitation? When they first walk in the room? What do I want them to hear, smell, see, touch, taste, and think? What do I want them to remember?" When you think this way, it sparks all kinds of creativity.

Second, *take time to plan your ceremony.* Try to begin planning a year in advance. It will give you time to be creative, and it will build anticipation and allow more people to participate. If you can't plan twelve months in advance, shoot for six.

Third, *invest money in your ceremony.* Meaningful ceremonies are costly, but they are worth it. Consider postponing a major purchase (car, furniture, sporting equipment) and instead put the money in a ceremony savings account. This is one of those times when cheaper isn't better. Be willing to budget or earn extra income to invest in your ceremony.

Fourth, *honor the individual.* We want to declare the value of the young man, celebrating who he is and who he is becoming. We want to declare his dignity, uniqueness, and worth.

Fifth, *make a lasting impression with symbols.* A meaningful symbol is critical for a memorable ceremony. What would a graduation be without a diploma? What would a wedding be without a wedding ring? A powerful symbol that has great significance is the cross. What are some ways you can use it in your ceremony?

Six, *highlight Scripture in a variety of ways.* What we say may have some permanence, but what God says has more permanence and certainly more power. Include Scripture readings, recitations, songs, artistic displays, and monuments that include God's Word. (For more on this, see Deuteronomy 6:4-9 and Joshua 4:1-7.)

Seven, *empower him with a hopeful future.* Powerful ceremonies celebrate a positive future and affirm the past. They are a gateway to a future strengthened by faith.

RESPONSE

1. It has been observed that teen boys like to cluster in a group of four to five in their "gang." In contrast, teen girls prefer a tighter group of two or three friends. What have you observed? Why is this?

2. What are parents to do with the double message of "stay away from me, but don't leave me?"

3. What are some of the ideals of manhood that boys need to develop to grow into maturity?

4. How would a rite of passage help a boy fill the void in his life?

5. Review and discuss the Seven Keys to a Memorable Ceremony.

A LETTER TO MY SON

Dear Son,

I am excited about planning some more rites of passage for you. I hope you like the ones that we have already done, remember?

▶ When we had the "funeral" for the training wheels for your bike? We buried them in the backyard and celebrated that you where on a "big-boy bike."

▶ When we had the special dinner the night before kindergarten, and we served your favorite meal and had a special school bus cake? You loved your gift of a new school outfit. We did something similar for your first day at elementary school and middle school.

▶ When you became a member of God's family? We gave you a new Bible with your name engraved on the front. When you got baptized, we gave you a gold cross and videotaped the event. At the lunch afterward, you received cards and gifts from family and friends who came to celebrate with us.

▶ When you graduated from fifth grade? I gave you a Swiss Army knife with all of the attachments and your name and a Scripture verse engraved on the side. I told you, "You are getting older and can be trusted. I trust you to use this wisely."

▶ In seventh grade, when you did the solo overnight in the mountains? We had prepared for months. You learned all of the necessary survival skills. You did it on your own, for twenty-four hours. I am proud of you!

Now you are in those exciting teenage years. I want to build more rites of preparation and confirmation with you.

Boys need to make a big deal out of going from one life stage to another. They want to celebrate it with others. When a boy doesn't get these rites of passage, he will often make his own. If his parents, family, and friends don't acknowledge and celebrate him, he will create artificial rites, like smoking, drinking, having sex, anything that can serve as a notch on his belt.

A boy needs a rite of passage. Just as a teenage girl has a monthly reminder that she is a female, a boy needs a regular reminder that he is on his journey to becoming a man.

I have listed below more ideas to serve as building blocks for rites of passage. Read them and see if you can come up with your own. Feel free to change the suggestions to make them more "you."

BASIC RITES OF PASSAGE

1. Develop a list of Wisdom Questions you want to ask your mentors. Any question is fair game.

2. Give away something that symbolizes your *old life.* You could give your childhood toys to charity.

3. Make a symbol that captures your spiritual growth: a fish, a cross, Scripture written on a rock, etc.

4. Customize your own car. Personalize it so it is different and unique.

5. Decorate your room in a way that reflects some of the ideals of manhood.

6. Go on a father-son outing to the store to purchase a razor, shaving cream, and a kit to keep it in.

7. Decide to serve your church. Instead of going only as a consumer, discover some way to help (teach a children's class, help serve coffee, do yard work, shovel snow).

I hope you like some of these ideas. I will look forward to discussing them, and the ones you suggest, this week when we meet.

Building a memory,
Dad

JOURNAL

Respond to the letter by writing your own thoughts in the section below. Parents may want to use Tim's letter as a model for their own.

_____

_____

_____

_____

_____

_____

_____

_____

_____

➡ CONNECTION ⬅

Plan a Rite of Passage
The key elements to a rite of passage are:
▶ Mentors
▶ Ordeals and Tests
▶ Rituals
▶ Community Celebration
▶ Gifts and Symbols

Write any ideas you would have for each of the elements. Then use the Monument Planner on page 227 to actually plan a Rite of Passage.

CHAPTER 34

A PREPARED YOUNG MAN

A male who reaches adulthood without learning a sacred role in life is not fully a man. He will wander through society without an internal compass by which to measure his worth in the society. One day he will be told that providing and protecting are good roles for him, and he'll agree. The next day he'll be told hands-on child care is the most important aspect of his role, and he'll agree. The next day he'll be told that meeting his wife's emotional needs is his most important job, and he'll agree. The next day he'll be told he's supposed to work himself to death, and he'll agree—until he wakes up one day and disagrees, confused and resentful.[1]

I like this quote from Michael Gurian's bestseller, *A Fine Young Man.* It captures what we want to discuss in this chapter. *Parents want to prepare teenagers for life,* but we don't simply want our teens to follow the trendy role of the month. We want to prepare them for life's situations. We want to help them respond wisely and responsibly.

Life Skills for Guys is designed to help young men prepare for life; to help each discover his sacred *role in life.* And in order to become a fine young man, a teen needs an internal compass.

We have a generation of young men without internal compasses. Our cafeteria culture says, "Choose your own rules," and "How can it be wrong if it feels so good?" Few things are considered sacred, so when someone says, "Discover your sacred role in life," it may be difficult to understand.

Think about a compass. It's not fancy. It does one thing and one thing only: it points north. Not south or west. Always north. Now this may not be very high tech or seem that impressive, until you are lost in the forest or trying to navigate in the fog on the open ocean. When you are lost or confused, the compass becomes very valuable. It points north. If you know how to use it, you can get to your destination. Lose your compass, or ignore what it tells you, and you risk your life.

We have a generation at risk because many kids don't have a moral compass, or they ignore theirs. What is a True North principle? *Something that is always right and true in all situations.* Sometimes these True North principles are called absolutes. You can count on them. They don't change with the weather, the stock market, or your team's win-loss record.

What is the source of these absolutes?

God's Word.

The best compass by which to evaluate all truth is God's written Word, the Bible. We can trust it because it is timeless; it's not going to change and be outdated tomorrow. We can trust it because it is universal. Biblical principles will apply in a variety of settings and cultures. We can trust it because it is inspirational. The Bible is not simply a collection of inspiring messages from religious dudes; it is the God-breathed Word of God.

God's Word is the ultimate source for True North principles.

For the compass to work, it must be read. If you are lost in the mountains and you have a compass, a topographic map, and are at the top of a scenic ridge, you have everything you need to find your way. But you have to do something with your information. The most expensive compass in the world won't help you unless you follow it. To benefit from True North principles, you have to read and follow the compass.

For a young man to have a sense of direction, he must *internalize* his compass. It's not enough to bring it, or look at it, or show it off: "Hey, look at my cool, stainless steel, designer compass!" For a compass to help a lost man, it must be followed. You have to do something with the information it shows you, taking the data into your life and acting on it. One of the big ideas behind *Life Skills* is that instead of having parents tell teens what to do, the parents help their kids discover principles that they can always believe in, and that become personal. These principles are a compass guiding each one along the way, helping teens make wise decisions *on their own.*

How important are these guiding principles?

The Search Institute has done extensive research in this area. They discovered forty developmental assets that have a huge impact on a teen's life.

> The institute's research has documented that the more assets a young person has, the less likely he or she is to engage in or experience a wide range of negative behaviors, including violence, early sexual intercourse, school problems and the use of alcohol and other drugs.[2]

In other words, if a teen has most of these assets in his life, he will be able to get through his teen years and be okay. But if he is lacking six or eight of them, he will be at risk. The forty assets were a source for the issues in the previous chapters in *Life Skills.* They deal generally with support, empowerment, boundaries, expectations, identity, social competencies, and commitment to learning.

The eighth area of assets incorporates *positive values.* This is the moral compass we have been talking about. The six True North values that a teen needs to be effective in life are:

▶ Caring—Placing high value on helping other people.

▶ Equality and social justice—Placing high value on promoting equality and reducing hunger and poverty.

▶ Integrity—Acting on convictions and standing up for your beliefs.

▶ Honesty—Telling the truth even when it is not easy.

▶ Responsibility—Accepting and taking personal responsibility.

▶ Restraint—Believing it is important not to be sexually active or to use alcohol or other drugs.[3]

Later on, we will see that each of these values is strongly supported by God's Word. If something is validated through scientific testing with thousands of teens, reinforced with personal experience, and clearly taught in Scripture, you can be sure that it is a True North principle, something you can base your life on.

RESPONSE

1. What do you think when you hear "a sacred role in life"?

2. What are some conflicting messages you receive about your role?

3. Have you had an experience with a compass? Describe it.

4. What are some True North principles that are important to you?

5. Take another look at the six positive values on page 205. How would each of these help you?

A LETTER TO MY SON

Dear Son,

As you know, each birthday we give you a unique gift. It isn't one that is purchased and wrapped; it is earned!

A gift that is earned? As you get older, we give you something to signify your maturing. We give you the gift of freedom with responsibility. It is a double-edged sword: with each year, you receive more freedom (you can stay up later), but you also receive more responsibility (like mowing the lawn).

This is a form of a rite of passage. "As you enter your thirteenth year, you now have the freedom to stay up to eleven P.M. on the weekends. Enjoy this new privilege. Along with this goes the responsibility of the thirteen-year-old—washing the van every Saturday. To commemorate this special occasion, I present you with this symbol of your new status." The boy is presented with a new bucket and matching sponge for use in his new responsibility. Sure, it might seem cheesy to some, but it gives you what you need: steps to manhood.

"It won't happen by accident." As parents, we are committed to deliberately passing on a strong heritage to our kids. That is why I am a leader with *Heritage Builders.* I want to intentionally prepare you to be a man. You won't evolve into a man. You won't become a man by accident. I don't think you will become a godly man, left to yourself and your natural bent. *You need a plan to become a man.*

When you were younger, your mom and I didn't know anything about the forty assets or other research indicating what kids need when they grow up. We just knew what we wanted to see in our kids, so we wrote it down. We defined the target—what kind of man we want you to be when you are eighteen. As far as I can see, you are well on the way.

THE TARGET: A PREPARED YOUNG MAN

▶ SPIRITUAL: To have a growing and vibrant faith in Christ.

▶ SOCIAL: To be able to make wise choices about friends and activities. To relate to a wide variety of people in diverse situations.

▶ PHYSICAL: To maintain good health and habits of an active lifestyle. To preserve your virginity until you are married. To practice a substance-abuse-free lifestyle.

▶ EMOTIONAL: To feel capable and confident in yourself and your God-given abilities. To draw boundaries, showing personal courage and not allowing others to take advantage of you.

▶ MENTAL: To be prepared for opportunities encountered in the future. To think critically and biblically with a Christian worldview.

▶ CHARACTER: To be honest, just, dependable, forgiving, compassionate, and generous.

▶ LIFE SKILLS: To develop skills in finances, vocational planning, ministry involvement, cooking, cleaning, car maintenance, and personal organization.

This last one was the original idea for this book!

Son, I know it's quite a list, but we also plan to stretch it out over the eighteen years or so that you live at home. Let's work on it together!

Do your best to present yourself to God as one approved, a workman who does not need to be ashamed and who correctly handles the word of truth (2 Tim. 2:15).

Love,
Dad

JOURNAL

Respond to the letter by writing your own thoughts in the section below. Parents may want to use Tim's letter as a model for their own.

_____

_____

_____

_____

_____

_____

_____

_____

➡ CONNECTION ⬅

Using the six True North principles, complete the following chart. Look up the Scripture and record how it relates to the value; then describe an activity that you could do for each. Choose three to work on. When you complete those, work on the next three.

Six Qualities I Need to Be a Godly Man:

Quality	Scripture	Activity
1. Caring	James 1:27	e.g. Give food to the homeless
2. Equality & Social Justice	James 2:1-10	_____
3. Integrity	Proverbs 11:3	_____
4. Honesty	Ephesians 4:22-25	_____
5. Responsibility	Galatians 6:7	_____
6. Restraint	1 Peter 4:1-8	_____

Option: Make an art project with these qualities as a reminder. Consider the theme "you need a plan to become a man." For instance, you could write these qualities on a blueprint. Blueprints are often available free at some graphics stores as rejects.

_____

1 Michael Gurian, *A Fine Young Man*, What Parents Mentors and Educators Can Do to Shape Adolescent Boys into Exceptional Men (New York: Jeremy P. Tarcher/Putnam, Inc., 1999) 244.
2 Nancy Leffert, Ph.D., Peter L. Benson, Ph.D., Jolene L. Roehlkepartain, *Starting Out Right* Developmental Assets for Children (Minneapolis, MN: Search Institute, 1997) 10.
3 Ibid. 99 (adapted).

CHAPTER 35

CELEBRATING WITH A BLESSING

F riday, 10:17 P.M.

BOOM-BOOM-BOOM . . . BOOM-BOOM-BOOM!

The banging of the drum interrupted the quiet night. Dogs began to bark. Neighbors turned on their porch lights and peered into the street.

"What's going on?" asked the startled thirteen-year-old boy. *It's bad enough having to go to bed at ten on a Friday, and now some clown is outside with a drum!*

"Mom! Who is it?" *Probably that nerdy neighbor and some of his buddies from the high school band. Real funny practical joke!* "MOM!"

Out on the lawn, below the boy's window, was a small assembly of men; one of them had a drum.

The boy turned out his bedroom light and stared into the darkness. He saw the man with the drum. Beside him stood a familiar figure holding a glowing camping lantern. *It's Dad! What is he up to?* "Mom, what is dad doing?"

Next to the boy's father were two men from the church and an older teenager, one of the men's son.

The drum stopped. Silence.

"Jared! Come out!" cried the boy's father.

Jared jumped back from his window. *Dad has lost it! He has stripped a gear.*

"Jared, come out!" he cried again.

BOOM-BOOM-BOOM . . . BOOM-BOOM-BOOM. . . BOOM-BOOM-BOOM!

Again the drumming ceased.

"JARED COME OUT!" the men's voice chorused in unison.

Jared squinted into the blackness. The Coleman lantern generated a yellow glow on the faces of the men. He noticed his dad's huge grin. *At least he's not mad now. He seemed mad when he told me to go to my room at ten. Now I know why. I wonder, what he is up to?* "What?" Jared shouted back at them.

"Really, Son. Come down now."

There was a knock on Jared's bedroom door.

"Come in."

His mom slowly opened the door.

POP! A flashing light blinded him. When his eyes focused, he saw his mom standing in his doorway, camera in hand.

"What are you trying to do? Scare me to death?"

"It's okay, Son. Go, be with your father and the men. Here—" She reached around the corner and produced his jacket. "Everything else you need is already in the van."

Jared grabbed his jacket and skipped down the stairs. He flung open the front door. The men were now standing on the front sidewalk.

"Leave your mother and come with us!" *BOOM!* "Leave your mother and come with us!" *BOOM!* "Leave your mother and come with us!" the men commanded in unison.

Jared stood in the doorway. He was uncertain about what lay ahead, but he knew these men; he knew his father. They could be trusted. He turned to kiss his mother good-bye, but for some strange reason, he decided not to. "See ya, mom," he said as he waved her off.

It would be a night he would always remember. It was his manhood ritual overnight. His head swirled with anticipation.

THE NEED FOR TRADITIONS

What would it be like to be Jared? Would you like it? Do you think it would be kind of weird? If you think it might be a little strange, I have to admit, it is. We don't see many examples of positive manhood traditions, and we greatly need meaningful traditions that are fun and memorable.

There are very few places in our culture where boys are intentionally initiated into manhood. Our boys are at a loss because they don't have these powerful, memorable experiences where, in the company of their father and other men, they can celebrate their steps to manhood. Because boys don't have these steps and ceremonies, they are left to wonder, *Am I a man?*

Sons delight in knowing about manhood. They have a hunger to know and be close to their father and other men. These sacred ceremonies have a unique way of bonding sons with their fathers. I will try to explain, but you really need to experience one to fully appreciate its impact.

Since 1992, I have been designing rites of passage that affirm boys and serve as stepping stones from childhood to manhood. What started as "a fun idea for a camping trip" has now expanded to be part of a national movement. In sharing some of the things we have learned, I hope it will help you plan your own celebration.

You deserve a celebration! If you have worked through all of *Life Skills* and did all those Connection activities (even the goofy ones!), you deserve some kind of big deal to celebrate.

So, what should we plan and why? Consider Robert Lewis' advice from his excellent book *Raising a Modern-Day Knight:*

> What is missing today in most father-son relationships? Why do the sons of even good, emotionally involved fathers drift in adulthood? Because we have forgotten to give them the best things! A social and spiritual competence can be summarized in three phrases:
> A vision for manhood,
> A code of conduct,
> A transcendent cause.[1]

Boys need a vision for manhood. In this book we have described the biblical view of what it means to be a man. We have also trained in the area of values and the importance of internalizing a code of conduct. As Christian men, we have a transcendent cause: we are servants of the King of kings.

We have the vision, the code, and the cause. Now, all we need is a ceremony!

TWO MANHOOD CEREMONIES

THE BLESSING RETREAT

In an observant Jewish home, children receive a daily blessing from their father. In the typical American home, most children grow up without a word of blessing from their parents their entire lives.

We are missing out on a significant opportunity.

In the times of the Old Testament, it was common for fathers to grant a blessing to their children. It was a time of affirmation and acceptance. It was more than saying *I love you;* it was a profound experience. A blessing could mean the difference between success and failure, between acceptance and rejection. We have a generation of young men hungry for a blessing from their parents.

The word *blessing* means *to bend the knee.* It represents the idea of honor or offering. Think of the Wise Men who knelt before Jesus and offered gifts. To bless someone means *to add to his or her life.* Basically, blessing means *to add,* and cursing means *to subtract.*

We have designed several Blessing Retreats for the sons and their parents in our church. They have been powerful and memorable experiences. (We also offer them for daughters.) The Blessing Retreat is based on Isaac's blessing to his sons as seen in Genesis 27. As you read this story, you will discover that there are five ways to demonstrate unconditional love to a child. I call these the five points of the blessing. They are easy to remember and spell out the word **B.L.E.S.S.**:

- ▶ **B**OND PHYSICALLY
- ▶ **L**IFELONG FRIENDSHIP
- ▶ **E**STEEM HIGHLY
- ▶ **S**POKEN WORD
- ▶ **S**PECIAL FUTURE

BOND PHYSICALLY

Young men need to have a parent's expression of affection. To bond physically means *to be connected and be comfortable expressing affection.* The time when a boy needs physical affirmation from his dad is the time most dads stop expressing physical affection. Some dads reason, *He is getting big now. I feel kind of funny. I'm not sure what I should do or not do.* So they stop the hugs, the tickles, the high-fives, and the wrestling. When they need it the most, many boys don't receive enough affection from their fathers.

On the Blessing Retreat, we send the boys on a walk with their parent. We encourage them to hold hands, walk closely, or put an arm on a shoulder when stopping to catch a breath or get a drink. Sometimes a touch can communicate volumes of love.

LIFELONG FRIENDSHIP

Making a commitment to relationship is the second point of the Blessing. It means to *invest in strengthening the relationship.* It is an agreement to stay connected through the various stages of life. It means that disagreements and conflicts will come, but we agree to work through them. This kind of commitment adds security to the teen-parent relationship. Teens go through a time of change and uncertainty. A commitment to a lifelong relationship from their parents helps them endure the challenges of adolescence.

In case you are wondering, guys, this does *not* mean you have to take your dad with you every time you go out! It doesn't mean you have to have your mom tag along when you go to the movies with your friends. When I say *friendship* with your parent, don't get nervous. I'm not trying to force your parent into your group of friends. What I am suggesting is that you consider a relationship with your parent which would eventually develop into a *friendship* when you are an adult. Does that make sense? It means laying the foundation now for a meaningful relationship later. It means building trust, making commitments, asking forgiveness, talking, encouraging each other, and giving each other time to grow.

On the Blessing Retreat, we direct the boys and their parents to look for symbols in nature that represent life-long connection. If we are in the mountains, we ask them to look for moss on a tree, or fruit or cones on a tree to represent dependency and connection. "A healthy pine tree makes pine cones. Right now you are like this pine cone, attached to the tree, but someday you will break away from me and generate new life. Until then, we are connected and benefit each other." Some guys have taken pine cones home as monuments.

One year, at the Father-Daughter Retreat, we were near the beach in Santa Monica—not too many pine cones around! We instructed the daughters and their dads to make their own monuments of a lifelong relationship. This is more of a challenge in a concrete jungle.

Bruce and his stepdaughter, Jen, enjoyed a walk on the beach and had gone through the five points of The Blessing, but they had not figured out how to make a memorial. They were so involved in their discussion, that as they walked across a parking lot, they didn't notice that it was recently oiled. They didn't notice it until they got to the next parking lot and their shoes made imprints on the dry surface. At first they were upset that they had ruined their brand new Nikes. Then, as they looked across the parking lot, they realized they had made their memorial. There, in stark contrast to the dry pavement, were two sets of footprints, close to each other, side-by-side for over one hundred feet of parking lot. They had made their monument! It represented to a stepfather and his stepdaughter their commitment to lifelong relationship: a dedication to walk together.

ESTEEM HIGHLY

Express love and respect for each other is the goal of the third point of The Blessing. To esteem highly is to consider the other person as more important than yourself. It is a way of saying, "How can I serve you?" and being a Christlike servant to your parent or teen.

Sometimes we suggest a foot-washing ceremony as part of the hike in order to show servanthood. Okay, this can be kind of gross. Feet get dirty and sweaty while on a hike, just like they did in Jesus' time. But as you kneel before someone and wash his feet, you are modeling love in the form of servanthood. *If you want to be great in God's kingdom, you have to be a servant.*

Another act of esteem is the Affirmation Acrostic. On the retreat, we have the parents secretly make these out of pieces of leather. Using the son's name, the parent creates an acrostic using the qualities they see and want to affirm. For instance if your son's name is Brad the acrostic might read:

B—Bright
R—Righteous (knows what is right and does it)
A—Accepting
D—Daring

Some choose to cut the leather into various shapes to represent something meaningful. With a Sharpie marking pen, the parents mark on the leather. The parent hides these until they are on the Blessing Walk and produces them as he or she affirms the son with the third point of the Blessing.

These are simple and affordable, but powerful, monuments. I have seen guys take these scraps of leather to college with them and place them prominently in their dorm room.

SPOKEN WORD

Words of encouragement and devotion are powerful. Isaac's mere words to Jacob altered his future. When Esau discovered that his brother had deceived his father and had manipulated his father's blessing, he cried out, "Bless me—me too, my father!" (Gen. 27:34).

We have a generation of young men who are pleading, "Me too, me too!" Just like a three year old who sees his older brother get picked up by their daddy and swung around, he wants the same experience. He will cry, "Me too, me too, Daddy!"

Parents, don't underestimate the power of your words. During this coaching period of life, your son needs words of encouragement. Just like a good coach who says, "You are doing better, keep working on this—" and then demonstrates how to improve, parents need to coach their sons with words.

Sons, you too can encourage your parent with what you say. Try a simple encouraging word to your mom or dad and see what happens.

It isn't enough to just have the feelings. It's like that dad who said, "I told him *I love you* when he was in preschool. Isn't that enough? I mean, I work hard to provide for him. Isn't that love?"

No. Not exactly. Our kids still need to hear words of love and affirmation.

On the Blessing Retreat, we encourage parents and sons to express words of affirmation to each other. *Spoken word* means *to affirm your son's character and personhood.* It means accepting him as a unique creation by God, affirming his individuality. Accept and honor him as a man.

We encourage parents to select a life verse to *speak into* their son's life and share this on their Blessing Walk. The verse can become their Scripture, one that reminds them of this shared time together and affirms certain qualities of their son. One parent chose Romans 15:13 to affirm hope, joy, peace, and faith in her son:

> May the God of hope fill you with all joy and peace as you trust in him, so that you may overflow with hope by the power of the Holy Spirit.

SPECIAL FUTURE

Faith applied to parenting. That is what the fifth point of The Blessing is all about. The parent is seeking to express his vision for a positive future to his son.

Our sons may ask, "What difference does being a Christian make?"

The answer: "We have a future and a hope." We can embrace the future, no matter what it holds, because we know God will walk with us.

Picturing a *special future* is to *create vision by expressing faith and hope.*

On our retreats, we ask sons and parents to hike to a place with a view. We ask them to sit down and talk about what they see. We instruct the parents to say something like, "Just as we can see a long way, I can imagine your future. I can picture a positive future for you as you walk with God. I can picture you as a man of God, one who passionately loves God and who demonstrates care to others. I am not sure what your career may be, but I can see you using your courage and your kind heart to really make a difference."

The point here is not to predict what the boy will *do,* but what he will *be.*

These life-affirming words of hope are powerful. They create a lasting impression of potential. The boy will begin to shape himself into the person his parent envisions. He will want to live up to the potential that his parent sees, according to his God-given potential as affirmed by the person who gave him life.

Many of our young men struggle with these questions: *What is a real man?* And, *Is it okay to be me?* Picturing a special future answers these basic questions that often restrict a boy from becoming all that he could be. Some of the struggles that young men in North America face would be minimized if they were to receive a blessing from their parents.

The basic question at the root of these problems is: *Am I worth anything?* To the young man who has received The Blessing, the answer is, "YES!"

CIRCLE OF BLESSING

At the conclusion of the retreat, we ask the sons to stand in a circle. Their fathers stand behind them, each with his right hand on his son's shoulder and his left hand on the father next to him.

"Welcome sons to the Circle of Brotherhood. We are all brothers in Christ. God is our Father. As a result of today's blessing, we no longer see you as boys. We see you as men—brothers in Christ."

"WELCOME SONS!" the fathers echo in unison.

"Now it is time to affirm our sons as men. Fathers, begin."

Each father speaks a word of affirmation and blessing to his son. The public declaration of acceptance and approval is compelling. Tears begin to roll. For some boys, this is the first time they have heard their dads affirm them.

"Now sons, it is your turn. As brothers in Christ, we are to affirm each other. A real man speaks encouraging words to another. It is your opportunity now to express appreciation for your father. Anything you want to say that affirms him is acceptable."

Now the tears really start to roll! This is a memorable time, because this is when a son reveals what he most appreciates about his dad.

"I liked my dad taking this time to come with me on this retreat."

"It meant a lot to me that my dad hugged me in front of all these men. He's not too macho to show he cares."

"We had fun hiking and skipping rocks across the water."

"Dad said things he never said before. I will never forget them."

"On our walk, my dad gave me this pocket knife and The Blessing. I know he means what he said."

THE CHRISTIAN BAR MITZVAH

Remember in chapter thirty-one where we introduced the idea of mentors and a Wisdom Council? Take another look at those concepts beginning on page 184. Much of what you will plan for your Christian Bar Mitzvah revolves around your Wisdom Council. The following is an abbreviated checklist to help you plan a meaningful ceremony honoring you as a Man of the Word (Christian Bar Mitzvah).

1. Decide on the qualities you want to develop in your life. Suggestion: use the thirty-four listed in this book (one from each chapter). Write them down. Commit yourself to working on them.

2. Recruit help! That's right, you can't do this alone. Decide on a small group of other guys, or start thinking of some mentors to serve on your Wisdom Council.

3. With your parent(s) help, recruit some mentors. Identify the four to seven qualities you want them to work on with you. Ask your mentors to affirm that they have observed these qualities in you at your Man of the Word ceremony.

4. Purchase a collapsible file from an office supply store. Use it to store records and ideas for your ceremony. Make the following tabs: budget, schedule, invitation list, invitations, Scripture, Wisdom Council, gifts and symbols, food, and site. File information under the appropriate tabs as you plan.

5. Begin meeting with your mentors. They may assign projects to help you develop the skill or quality you desire. Remind them that they will present a short talk at your ceremony.

6. Reserve a location and decide on what you will do for food. Some guys have it catered and others have it potluck. The important thing is that the food preparation and service doesn't get in the way or distract from your ceremony.

7. Arrange for a master of ceremonies and all of the technical requirements for the room (set-up, sound equipment, VCR, etc.)

8. Select or design your own invitations. Prepare the list. Review with your parents.

9. Send out the invitations with an RSVP. Collect and plan on your number. Add 10 percent for late responses.

10. Design your program. It might look like this:

Sunday Afternoon: *Man of The Word Bar Mitzvah*
3:45 P.M. Instrumental background music playing

4:00 P.M. Special music by one of your friends

4:05 P.M Welcome and explanation of the ceremony—MC

4:10 P.M. Scripture reading—friend or youth worker

4:15 P.M. Video montage of key events in your life

4:20 P.M. Wisdom Council mentors (3-5 minutes each). Each mentor affirms one skill or quality in you, shares about the mentoring experience, offers a Scripture verse presented in a frame or mounted, optional gift.

4:40 P.M. Your presentation (responding to your mentors, your favorite experience, your favorite verse, etc.)

4:50 P.M. Parental Blessing (optional gift such as leather, name-engraved Bible)

4:55 P.M. Prayer of Blessing (Pastor or one of the mentors). You kneel and the mentors lay hands on you and pray.

5:00 P.M. Refreshments or meal

11. Within a few days after the ceremony, send thank-you cards to all who participated or helped.

Ask for the speaking notes from your mentors and place them in a scrapbook that will commemorate your day. Add photos and other memorabilia.

A new relationship between teen and parent is formed through this rite of passage. The young man is given more responsibility in vital areas: his own quiet times, helping to lead Family Nights, choosing relationships, choosing activities, learning from mentors and being accountable to them. A new level of honor and respect is established between teen and parent.

There you have it! A step-by-step approach to a Christian Bar Mitzvah. If you really want to get into it, there are manuals at your local bookstore that tell how to plan a Jewish Bar Mitzvah. You can purchase one of these and adapt it for your family. Be creative and don't worry about being "wrong." There are so few of these rites of passage that nobody knows what to expect!

RESPONSE

1. What has been a memorable ceremony in your life?

2. What do you think about a Christian Bar Mitzvah? What would you

change? Would you use a Wisdom Council?

3. Review the five points of The Blessing. Discuss which would be the most rewarding to you (parent and teen).

4. What do you think would be the impact on a young man who received The Blessing?

5. Review Seven Keys to a Memorable Ceremony (page 199) Use these to plan your ceremony.

JOURNAL

Respond to the letter by writing your own thoughts in the section below. Parents may want to use Tim's letter as a model for their own.

_____

_____

_____

_____

_____

_____

_____

➡ CONNECTION ⬅

As a teen/parent team, design a Bar Mitzvah or Blessing event. For additional help, see the Guide to a Blessing Walk and The Blessing Covenant in the Appendix. To help you develop an Affirmation Acrostic, refer to the alphabetized qualities, also in the Appendix.

---

1 Robert Lewis, *Raising a Modern-Day Knight*, A Father's Role in Guiding His Son to Authentic Manhood (Wheaton, IL: Tyndale House Publishers, 1997) 39.

APPENDIX A

CONTRACT FOR LIFE

A Foundation for Trust and Caring

By agreeing to this contract, we recognize that SADD encourages all young people to adopt a substance-free lifestyle. We view this contract as a means of opening the lines of communication about drinking, drug use, and traffic safety to ensure the safety of all parties concerned. We understand that this contract does not serve as permission to drink, but rather, a promise to be safe.

Young Adult: I acknowledge that the legal drinking age is 21 and have discussed with you and realize both the legal and physical risks of substance use, as well as driving under the influence. I agree to contact you if I ever find myself in a position where anyone's substance use impairs the possibility of my arriving home safely. I further pledge to maintain safe driving practices at all times, including wearing my safety belt every time and encouraging others to do the same.

_____
Signature

Parent/Guardian: Upon discussing this contract with you, I agree to arrange for your safe transportation home, regardless of time or circumstances. I further vow to remain calm when dealing with your situation and discuss it with you at a time when we are both able to converse calmly about the matter.

I agree to seek safe, sober transportation home if I am ever in a situation where I have had too much to drink or a friend who is driving me has had too much to drink. Recognizing that safety belt usage is a vital defense against death and injury on the highway, I promise to wear my safety belt at all times and encourage others to do the same.

_____
Signature

_____
Date

(Reproduced from Students Against Driving Drunk, Marlboro, MA. Used by permission.)

THE BLESSING IS PASSED ON

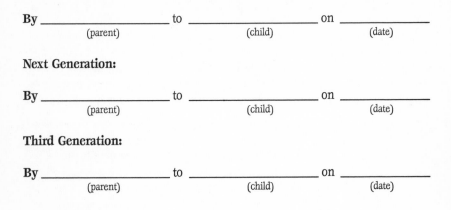

By _____ to _____ on _____
      (parent)   (child)   (date)

Next Generation:

By _____ to _____ on _____
      (parent)   (child)   (date)

Third Generation:

By _____ to _____ on _____
      (parent)   (child)   (date)

Love the Lord your God with all your heart and all your soul and with all your strength. These commandments that I give you today are to be upon your hearts. Impress them on your children. Talk about them when you sit at home and when you walk along the road, when you lie down and when you get up. Tie them as symbols on your hands and bind them on your foreheads. Write them on the door frames of your houses and on your gates. . . . Know therefore, that the Lord your God; He is the faithful God, keeping his covenant of love to a thousand generations of those who love him and keep his commands (Deut. 6:5-9, 7:9)

PRAYER OF BLESSING

"Lord, I thank You for _____. I thank You that he is Your child. May he love You with all of his heart, and all of his soul and all of his strength.

May _____'s focus in life be on You, Lord. I commit myself to him and to You, God, to walk with him on his journey. To talk about You. To take time for the truly important things. May he know and feel my love and support. I thank You, God, for the hopeful future You have planned for him. Bless _____ with a heart of pure devotion for You. Protect him from anything that would keep him from becoming the man of God You want him to be."

Amen

THE BLESSING WALK
Father & Son Retreat

PURPOSE: To provide an environment for fathers to affirms their sons with the Biblical rite of **The Blessing**.

FIVE POINTS OF THE BLESSING	PROJECT	POSITION
Bond Physically	Meaningful touch is a way to communicate warmth, personal acceptance and connection	Father, place hands on son's shoulders or hold his hand.
	Find a seed, a pod, or some fruit that shows connection to a plant (i.e., kelp). Say, "Son, I always want you to remember that we're in this together. You're part of me and I'm part of you. We're together."	
Lifelong Relationship	Look at the waves. Say, "Notice how the waves continually roll in. You can always count on them coming this way. I want you to always be able to count on me. I want a lifelong relationship with you."	Your choice
Esteem Highly	Take a wood block and marking pen (we provide). Make a monument of affirmation. Using your son's name as an acrostic, write words that will describe him and build	Pick a landmark that you can return to—a tree, pier, etc. This will serve as a special monument as well.

him up. Example:

Devoted
Able
Noble

Special Future

Option A: Find an object
Option A: Find an object   Your Choice
to symbolize a positive
future. (i.e. bud of new
growth, baby sand crabs,
etc.) Say, "Just as this bud
has a future of hope and
potential, I believe you
do, too."

Option B: Draw a line in
the sand at the tide line.
Watch the waves wash
over it. Say, "The tide is
going in/out. We know it
always does. Tomorrow it
will, and the net day. In
10 years the tide will be
the same. I believe in you
too and picture you living
a life of purpose and help
to others. Now, next week
and 10 years from today."

Spoken Word

Keep the *parchment bless-*   Some place you can com-
ing hidden until now.   fortably sit for at least 10
Have it completed ahead   minutes.
of time. Unroll it and
read it to your son.
Encourage him to pass it
on to his children.
Optional: You may
choose to review the five
points of *The Blessing*,
ending with prayer.

APPENDIX D

HOW TO BUILD MONUMENTS (MEMORIALS) IN YOUR LIFE

1. Journal your spiritual journey
2. Make a memorial of your first spiritual decision.
3. Discover your spiritual gift, then acknowledge and use it.
4. Share your spiritual journey with someone.
5. Seek a "mountain" or a lonely place to meet God.
6. Celebrate your spiritual birthday.
7. Pilgrimage to your spiritual roots. Visit places that are meaningful.
8. Write a note of appreciation to those who have shaped or are shaping your spiritual heritage.
9. Read a book on personal spiritual growth or disciplines or a Christian biography. Sign and date it when you begin "What I hope to get" and end "What I received from this book."
10. Record your prayers and God's answers in a blank book.
11. Make a collage of your walk with God.
12. Write a song that expresses your heart for God.
13. Spiritual life line (timeline)—chronology of spiritual growth.
14. Record milestones, goals, and barriers for your spiritual growth in your journal or daily organizer.
15. Develop a blueprint for building your life.
16. Make a flag or banner that celebrates something meaningful in your spiritual growth.
17. Design a Coat of Arms that represents what legacy you'd like to live for and pass on.
18. Play "I Spy." Note God at work (record these in a secret spy book).
19. Keep mementos that mean something to you.
20. Develop a Personal Mission Statement and display it prominently.

APPENDIX E

MONUMENT PLANNER

Event: Date/Age

Name of Teen:

Purpose of Event:

Scriptural Purpose:

Theme and Scripture:

Symbols and Gifts: What they represent:

People to include in planning: What each will do:

People to Invite:

Schedule:

Budget:

APPENDIX F

CHARACTER ATTRIBUTES

A	admirable	attentive	accomplished	able	amazing
B	bold	believer	brave	blessing	buddy
C	concerned	conscientious	courageous	confident	creative
D	disciplined	determined	discerning	decisive	devoted
E	expectant	energetic	enthusiastic	enjoyable	effective
F	flexible	faithful	forgiving	firm	flair
G	good	gentle	grateful	giving	gracious
H	honorable	harmonious	humble	helpful	happy
I	inquisitive	interested	important	intelligent	incredible
J	joyful	jubilant	just	jazzy	jester
K	kind	kingly	keen	kooky	knowledgeable
L	loyal	leader	listener	loving	lively
M	merciful	mindful	mature	merry	manly
N	noble	neat	nifty	nutty	natural
O	obedient	observant	orderly	organized	obvious
P	prepared	peaceful	protective	patient	pleasing
Q	quick	quiet	quality		
R	responsible	reliable	resourceful	reputable	reverent
S	servant	special	smart	strong	self-controlled
T	thoughtful	teachable	temperate	thankful	truthful
U	unique	upright	useful	understanding	
V	victorious	valuable	virtuous	visual	vital
W	wise	watchful	witness	wonderful	worthy
X	"x-cellent"	"x-traordinary"	"x-treme"		
Y	yearning	young	yourself		
Z	zealous	zippy	zany	zestful	